WE SURVIVED
THE END OF
THE WORLD

WE SURVIVED THE END OF THE WORLD

LESSONS FROM NATIVE AMERICA ON APOCALYPSE AND HOPE

STEVEN CHARLESTON

Broadleaf Books
Minneapolis

WE SURVIVED THE END OF THE WORLD
Lessons from Native America on Apocalypse and Hope

Library of Congress Cataloging-in-Publication Data

Names: Charleston, Steven, author.
Title: We survived the end of the world : lessons from Native America on apocalypse and hope / Steven Charleston.
Description: Minneapolis : Broadleaf Books, [2023].
Identifiers: LCCN 2022056300 (print) | LCCN 2022056301 (ebook) | ISBN
   9781506486673 (hardback) | ISBN 9781506486680 (ebook)
Subjects: LCSH: Indian philosophy--North America. |
   Uncertainty--Psychological aspects. | Survival--Psychological aspects. |
   Disasters--Psychological aspects.
Classification: LCC E98.P5 C45 2023 (print) | LCC E98.P5 (ebook) |
DDC 191.089/97--dc23/eng/20230105
LC record available at https://lccn.loc.gov/2022056300
LC ebook record available at https://lccn.loc.gov/2022056301

Cover design: Jay Smith—Juicebox Designs
Cover image: Federica Grassi

Print ISBN: 978-1-5064-8667-3
eBook ISBN: 978-1-5064-8668-0

To Susan
I could not have survived without you.

CONTENTS

1

APOCALYPSE
The Mystery and Miracle of Survival

The mystical theme of the space age is this: the world as we know it is coming to an end. The world as the center of the universe, the world divided from the heavens, the world bound by horizons in which love is reserved for members of the in-group: that is the world that is passing away. Apocalypse does not point to a fiery Armageddon but to the fact that our ignorance and our complacency are coming to an end.

—Joseph Campbell

WHEN I WAS six years old, I was taught to hide under my desk at school in the event of an atomic explosion. As ridiculous as it may seem now, this exercise was practiced throughout this country. This was in the early 1950s, during the Cold War, a standoff between the United States and the

Soviet Union (Russia). Both sides were armed with nuclear weapons, and the threat of their use was always a possibility. Consequently, a sense of dread hung over my childhood. The end of the world seemed just around the corner.

We are still hiding under our desks, waiting for the big one to drop. As a society, we are still living in anxiety. We are still afraid. Only now we have much more than nuclear war to worry about. We have global pandemics. We have social turmoil. We have irreversible environmental collapse. More than that, we face these threats while coping with our own personal issues: family troubles, illness, financial struggles. The combined weight of all these realities can push us to the brink of despair. It feels like we are living in a time of apocalypse, an age when everything we take for granted is starting to collapse around us. It feels like the end of the world.

In this book, I invite us to crawl out from under our desks—to stand up to face our challenges without fear and to discover new spiritual ways to cope with times of trouble. This situation is nothing new for me as a Native American. My ancestors already lived through an apocalypse. For us, the end of the world is "been there, done that."

In 1831, the world came to an end for my family—and for all the families that were part of Chahta Yakni, the Choctaw Nation. That year, we were forced off our ancestral homeland and made to walk on a death march we called the Trail of Tears. Thousands of our people died. We lost our homes, our way of life, even our graveyards. We lost everything—everything, that is, except the one thing they could not take from us: hope.

This book has grown from that seed: the idea that people can survive an apocalypse. How they do so is the vision at the heart of this book. My ancestors are a case study in survival. Not the grim survival of bunkers and bomb shelters, but the liberating and hopeful survival of a spiritual community. Native American culture in North America has been through the collapse of civilization and lived to tell the tale. My goal is to investigate how my ancestors were able to do that—and what their experience can teach all of us who are living in uncertain times.

But first, we need to be on the same page with our use of the word *apocalypse*. What does it mean, and how will we use it in this book? While many of us equate apocalypse with catastrophe or even with the end of the world, that is actually only half of the meaning. In Greek, the word derives from *apokaluptein*, which means to "uncover" or "reveal." Originally the word meant a vision of the future, a revelation about what was to come. The last book in the Christian New Testament is called the book of Revelation. It is the vision of the end time—the cataclysmic transformation of reality—at least as seen by the first-century mystic who composed it.

In fact, it was the writer of the book of Revelation who gave the word its second meaning by describing that transformation in such graphic and fantastic imagery. Over time, people began to interpret the meaning of apocalypse not only as a visionary revelation but an actual event. The two definitions began to merge. In Europe, for example, from 1346 to 1353, a pandemic known as the Black Death moved slowly across the continent, killing millions of people. People in the path of the plague saw it as an apocalyptic revelation of God's anger at them. They understood it as a message, a warning, from heaven. And once the plague arrived in their area, they saw its devastation firsthand and interpreted it as the end of their world. In this way, *apocalypse* became a term to describe both a vision of what is to come and a description of what is already happening.

The word *apocalypse* is now used to describe disasters of all kinds, including the Hollywood vision of a zombie apocalypse. As we will see later in this book, it can also describe our own personal apocalypse: an emotional, financial, or health crisis within our own lives. It is a popular shorthand term for total destruction. In this book we will use the word *apocalypse* with both meanings: a vision and an event. We will understand that the two meanings describe a process. The two meanings work together like an engine: the vision of an impending apocalypse is the fuel, and the actual events of an apocalypse are the combustion. When people are anxious about their future, when they see storm clouds on the horizon, they speak of an impending disaster waiting to happen. This apocalypse is a revelation of what is to come. Then, when it does happen, the apocalypse embodies the predicted event.

Apocalypse is what we are living through. It is the coming true of our worst fears, which in turn generates more visions, either of salvation or destruction. In human history we can trace how this process has unfolded over and over. Cassandra-like prophets rise up to warn us of a coming disaster. They suggest how it will happen and why. Then the prophesied event either occurs or fails to happen, and the process of apocalyptic thinking repeats itself. This process takes place throughout history and in all cultures and faith traditions. The revelation of an end time is universal. Like the story of the great flood, which appears in many religions and cultures, it is a common spiritual theme for humanity, something we have all experienced.

Conquest, war, famine, and death: the four horsemen of the apocalypse are still with us, both as fear and experience. Today we live in an age of anxiety. We are in that part of the apocalyptic process where wars and rumors of wars abound, where we watch the specter of environmental collapse coming at us with what seems like unstoppable certainty; where institutions on which we have always relied are starting to wobble and crumble; and where disease can reach pandemic proportions that we struggle to control or contain. Consequently, millions of people sense an apocalyptic dread rising up around them. Perhaps you are one of them.

— • —

It was the experience of apocalypse, not just the fear of it, that my ancestors faced. On Turtle Island, the name many Indigenous nations give to North America, the apocalypse began its inexorable consuming of our Indigenous way of life from the moment European settlers reached our shores. Our people died from a host of diseases for which they had no immunity or cure. The *Mayflower* was a plague ship. It, and the countless others like it, brought smallpox, measles, and influenza—diseases we had never known before that wiped out whole communities to the last person. At the same time European colonialism, with its rapacious hunger for our land, brought war and destruction upon us no matter how many peace treaties we signed. Whatever we gave, it was never enough. Many of us were forced onto death marches, like the Trail of Tears, that claimed the lives of thousands of people, especially our elders and infants.

Over time, our children were taken from us. They were taken to boarding schools where they suffered physical and sexual abuse. They were forbidden to speak their language or wear their cultural styles of hair or clothing. The animals on which we relied for food were systematically slaughtered and left to rot. Racism made us objects of derision and scapegoating. Even our ways of prayer and worship were outlawed. We were left in poverty and isolation, with the expectation that our genocide would soon be complete.

If you wanted to find an experiential example of an apocalypse, you would be hard pressed to find one more total than what North America's Indigenous civilization confronted for more than four hundred years. If apocalypse means cataclysmic destruction—in essence, an end of the world—my ancestors went through it.

But they did not all die. They did not become victims of genocide. They did not disappear. They survived. Even if only as a remnant of what once had been, they came through the nightmare to live another day.

How? That's the question this book seeks to answer. And finding the answer is crucial for all of us who worry that we are sleepwalking toward other pandemics, other wars, other times of corruption and cruelty. What enabled Native American communities to withstand the devastating blow of European colonialism, with all its death and fury? How did they achieve the miracle of their own survival? What can we learn from America's Indigenous people that may not only help us to endure an apocalypse but, even more importantly, prevent one from happening? Given my ancestors' experience, there are no better teachers in all the world on this subject.

Looking for an answer begins with apocalypse as revelation. An uncovering. A discovery. A vision. Rather than being mesmerized by the actual events of the American Apocalypse—the term I will use to describe the historical experience of North America's Indigenous nations—I began my search in the realm of revelation. What did the American Apocalypse reveal about my ancestors? What did it uncover about their survival? Where did their strength come from?

What I call the apocalyptic process happened here in North America just as it has in other global communities. When the early Christians, for example, who lived in the first century after the death of Jesus, saw an apocalypse gathering over them like a storm, when the persecutions and killings began, they turned to apocalypse as revelation, looking for a vision of a future they could still hope for and believe in. They turned to people like the mystic who wrote the book of Revelation. They turned to their prophets.

I decided to do the same thing. In trying to discern how and why my ancestors lived through one of the greatest human cataclysms in history, I decided to rediscover the prophets of my people: the prophets who had seen it coming and who, once it arrived with a vengeance, helped their people live through it with courage and dignity. I followed the path of apocalyptic revelation to uncover the mystery and miracle of Native American survival. I listened once again to the voices of Native American prophets to discover what they could teach me about the world in which we live today.

— • —

In the end, I found what I was looking for. But before I share it, I need to say a word about the prophets themselves. Prophets do not arise out of a vacuum. They are part of the apocalyptic process. They appear first as an early warning system within any culture at risk. They fulfill the classic role of the prophet as herald of a vision of what is to come. Then, as the apocalypse becomes ever more real, they serve as teachers to instruct people about what to do to end the suffering and alter the course of destruction. Finally, they are mystics who describe the future and guide people to find it within themselves.

In carrying out these roles in the apocalyptic process, the prophet strives to stand on solid ground, even while the earth beneath their feet is moving. That is, prophets not only talk about the future but the past. They ground their prophecy in the bedrock spiritual traditions of their people. They recall the ancient stories and covenants between the divine and human beings. They reinterpret ancient teachings and remind people of old promises. Prophets are immersed in tradition even as they talk about how that tradition will need to change to meet new apocalyptic challenges.

In Native America, that spiritual tradition is as deep and rich as any culture on earth. Native American prophets who arose during the worst years of our suffering stood in a spiritual history thousands of years old. Their messages, therefore, need to be understood in context—not only in the apocalyptic context of historical colonialism, but in the even older context of Native American religious ritual and practice. A prime example of this is the importance of songs and dances in all Native American prophecy.

Imagine if the writer of the book of Revelation had not used written words to convey the vision, but instead had composed a song to be sung and dance steps to be followed by all those who wanted to understand the prophecy. That is what is distinctive about Native American apocalyptic prophecy: it was interactive. People not only read or heard the prophecy, they physically participated in it. They embodied it in sacred dances.

Each of the prophets I have selected to explore in this book believed deeply in their ancient traditions, and each created songs and dances as a bridge between those ancient beliefs and the demands of a new reality. It would not be wrong to say that my ancestors sang and danced their way through the apocalypse, physically moving from one reality to the next.

Another aspect of the prophets I have followed in this book is that they were all very human and very much a part of their own time. These are not semidivine personages, but men and women with all their shortcomings and frailties exposed to full view. As it happens, in this work I have chosen four men—not because there were no female prophets but because, as so often happens to women in history, when men were in charge of recording events, they often ignored or diminished the story of women.

It is critical to emphasize that a great number of women played key roles in Native America's apocalyptic process. We have names for some of these women prophets. Some were important contemporaries of the male prophets we will examine—for example, Beata of the Delaware and Coacoochee of the Mohawk were part of the pivotal conflicts leading up to the War of 1812. Other women of this era were not only visionaries but active military leaders, such as Nanye-hi of the Cherokee. Lozen was a spiritual prophet for the Chiricahua Apache nation. And there was Kauxuma nupika of the Kutenai nation on the Columbia Plateau, who was part of the Dreamer religion that we will explore in chapter 4. Kauxuma was a two-spirit prophet, born a biological woman but returned from the vision quest as a male.

All these women, and many more like them, were clearly respected in their own community. In fact, in all Indigenous nations, women were integral to apocalyptic prophecy. In many cases, male prophets emerged from matrilineal cultures in which female leaders were instrumental in developing both the spiritual tradition and the new prophetic tradition. Women were pivotal in every case we explore in this book. Hopefully, in the years to come, more scholarship will reveal a deeper appreciation for their contributions to history.

The submersion of the female prophetic voice is due to the prejudice and misogyny of those Europeans who recorded both apocalyptic events and revelations as they were occurring. The women were bypassed for the men—although even then, the record of the male prophets often has a dismissive tone. All the prophets I include here were called fakers, frauds, conmen, drunks, madmen, and savages. During their lifetimes they were dismissed as charlatans who were stirring up the "hostiles" and rejecting the true religion of the missionaries. All suffered and struggled for what they said, and all of them died in relative obscurity.

In lifting up their names again, I can only pull them partially from that obscurity, because this book is not intended to be a work of history, especially since that history has been dominated by the interpretation of white scholars. I will be as generous as I can in the time and space I give to describing their experience and their teachings, but my primary goal will be to interpret their story from the Native American spiritual context. What did they teach us about how to survive an apocalypse? What cultural elements of their vision can be translated into our contemporary situation? How can we pull insights from the colonial history written by settler scholars to form a new understanding of who these people really were and what their message means for all of us?

But first we need to lay the foundation of the four prophets. They are Ganiodaiio of the Seneca, Tenskwatawa of the Shawnee, Smohalla of the Wanapams, and Wovoka of the Paiute. Each of these prophets was unique to his own culture, but they also shared many similarities. In the beginning, before their mission of prophecy began, they were considered fairly unremarkable by their communities—and in some cases, less than unremarkable. One was blind in one eye, and another was bent by scoliosis. Ganiodaiio and Tenskwatawa were both severely alcoholic in their younger years, almost to the point of death. Both were brought back to life by a profound apocalyptic vision. They all lived in traditional ways, but they also challenged their traditions to change in order to deal with the collapse of civilization as they knew it. They all lived and taught during times of war. Their experiential reality was that mixture of racism, disease, and conflict that I describe as the American Apocalypse. They were spiritual medics seeking to heal their people even in the midst of battle.

These four prophets taught through oral tradition. They did not write down their visions in a document like the book of Revelation; their words were recorded by others and passed on by word of mouth. In the case of Ganiodaiio, those words were eventually collected into a text: the Gaiwiio, a code of teachings to follow and ceremonies to do that became the basis of a religious practice that continues to this day. Much of what we know from the others was transcribed from their speeches at treaty negotiations or during public gatherings. Wovoka, for example, was interviewed on several occasions. All of them had their spiritual movements described and often denigrated in newspaper stories at the time or in reports from political or military figures trying to suppress their visions.

All four of these prophets were considered subversive by the colonial powers of their time, either the British or the Americans. They were suspected of fomenting resistance against white settlement of Native American land. They were thought of as radicals. Therefore, their teachings went underground. Their messages were kept secret, especially in situations where discovery could mean death.

Followers of both Tenskwatawa and Wovoka, for example, were massacred by the American military for their faith.

Even though much of the vision of these four Native American prophets was obscured, either by propaganda against them or by the design of their own followers to protect themselves, the medium through which their words were preserved—oral tradition—was a powerful and effective tool for the transmission of information in apocalyptic times. The message of Ganiodaiio, for example, had been memorized by different people in different communities; when these memories were recorded, they turned out to be nearly identical. While we must read between the lines to find the heart of what each prophet taught, we can do so with some assurance that we are recovering the original vision of the prophet himself. As late as 1924, for example, when Wovoka was older, he was invited by a Hollywood star to visit the outdoor set of a Western movie. When he arrived, the Native Americans who had been hired as extras for the movie gathered around him and showed him great reverence, because they had all heard of his teachings and they remembered what he had said.

Our task, in this book, will be to try to remember too. Not exhaustively. Not in detail, for this is not a book about colonial history or Native American leaders. This is a project in the apocalyptic process. We will sketch the outlines of the context in which each prophet lived, and then we will explore their response as spiritual visionaries. We will try to connect the dots. We will look for themes at the heart of the Native American vision that we can apply to our own situation in these days of struggle. Our primary goal will be to distill the deepest wisdom of their revelation as it shines light on our own hopes and fears. We will seek to bring their witness into the prophetic process, to let it uncover again the realities of apocalypse as we are experiencing them, and to offer us guidance, support, and inspiration for the days to come.

— • —

In the end, this book will be less about the four prophets and more about those of us who need their teachings now more than ever before. We want them to do for us now what they once did for their own communities: show us the path through apocalyptic fear to the revelation of a new apocalyptic hope. For hope will have the last word in this book.

Beyond the four individual prophets, we will learn from the collective apocalyptic vision of a whole Indigenous culture: the Hopi. This is not the teaching of a single prophet, but of a people as prophets. The Hopi people of the American Southwest have maintained a culture of apocalyptic process for centuries. They have seen the end of the world many times and chronicled their ancestors' journey to survival. They have watched the signs of prophecy unfolding in the earth and in the stars. They have developed spiritual practices that maintain the balance of all creation and that preserve life on this planet. The chapter following the discussion of the four prophets will be a deep dive into the mysticism of the Hopi so we can learn from them about the ultimate meaning of the cycles of life.

Like the four prophets, the Hopi have been both revered and maligned. They have had their message coopted and misinterpreted by others, often on purpose or for financial gain. Consequently, like the four prophets, they have kept their teachings underground and secret. In considering their wisdom we will approach their prophecy with respect and humility. We are not here to be spiritual voyeurs. We will not try to strip-mine or appropriate their culture to find what we want for ourselves. Instead we will do with the Hopi exactly what we do with the four prophets: consider the context, listen to the response, interpret the meaning. Our goal will not be to encompass Hopi tradition in our own privileged position, for this is not a book about the Hopi; rather, it will be to pay attention to what the Hopi are willing to share that we may learn from them some lessons to inspire our own journey.

The purpose of my following the path of these four Native American prophets and the Hopi tradition is to perform an act of apocalyptic revelation: to uncover what they understood then that can help us now. In doing this, I will take my part in the apocalyptic process. Over the next pages I will try to reveal the role of each prophet. I will present the historical context in which they lived and summarize their response to it. Then, as all prophets do, I will try to interpret their spiritual message for all of us, for a diverse community facing an apocalypse in our own time. In fact, I will go beyond the four individual prophets themselves to seek a Native American revelation that both encompasses and transcends all the messages we will examine in this book. In terms of Native American apocalyptic prophecy, I will seek to go a step beyond. I will search for a vision that can help us prevent the disaster we fear.

Finally, in the closing chapter, I will do something I have not done before. I will take the risk of any prophet by offering my own vision. I will seek to summarize what I have learned from the four prophets and from the Hopi. I will try to reveal the nature of the apocalypse we are facing and suggest how we can prevent it from taking us where none of us wish to go. Instead, I will show us a path to the world to come that is both hopeful and healing.

Apocalypse is both event and vision. It is a process that recurs time after time in human history. It is a description of reality and an invitation to imagine a different reality—a reality coming to be. It is revelation: an uncovering of our worst fears and highest aspirations. It is a look back, and it is a step forward. My ancestors lived this process, both in real time and in end time. They died and were reborn, just as the Native American prophets in these pages describe their own visionary experience.

The Indigenous people of North America endured one of the greatest and cruelest onslaughts in human history. They went through the end of their world. Today we may be afraid that something like that may happen to us. We may watch the signs of the times and feel insecure, aware that when the great tides of change shift, they do not always shift for the better. Pandemics, environmental destruction, corrupt governments, war, and natural disasters: my ancestors have been through it all before. They have survived, and they have returned to the land of the living. They bring a message of hope and transformation. They offer a vision of healing and restoration. They have something to tell us about how apocalypse works.

They can lead us to discover not only how to live through difficult times, but how to change the course of history to prevent the worst from happening. They have an answer. Our goal, in this book, is to learn that answer—and then, even more importantly, to live by it.

2

GANIODAIIO
A Plain Pathway before Me

He made mistakes, many mistakes, so it is reported, but he was only a man and men are liable to commit errors. Whatever he did and said of himself is of no consequence. What he did and said by the direction of the four messengers is everything—it is our religion. Ganiodaiio was weak in many points and sometimes afraid to do as the messengers told him. He was almost an unwilling servant. He made no divine claims, he did not pose as infallible nor even truly virtuous. He merely proclaimed the Gaiwiio and that is what we follow, not him. We do not worship him, we worship one great Creator. We honor and revere our prophet and leader, we revere the four messengers who watch over us—but the Creator alone do we worship.

—Cornplanter, brother of the prophet

IF YOU HAD been born in the time and place where Hadawa'ko was born, an apocalypse would be the last thing on your mind. When he was born, his people were at the apex of their cultural stability and influence. Hadawa'ko—also known by the honorific name Ganiodaiio and best known by the English translation of his name, Handsome Lake—was born into the great Haudenosaunee (Iroquois) Confederacy in 1735. He was born into the Seneca Nation, the Keepers of the Western Door, whose ancestral lands were throughout the Finger Lakes in central New York and in the Genesee Valley in western New York. Along with their allied nations—the Oneidas, Onondagas, Cayugas, Mohawks, and Tuscaroras—the Seneca in 1735 were part of a large, stable, and prosperous culture.

The Haudenosaunee lived together under the Great Law of Peace, a precursor to the American Constitution brought to the people by two great prophets of peace, Deganawidah and Ayonwantha (also known as Hiawatha). Their form of government became a model that other nations, such as the United States, would copy and seek to emulate. It was a balance of authority not only between the Native nations themselves but between the roles of men and women within the society. While there was no sense of land ownership as the Europeans understood it, land and homes were passed down the female line, so women had material security. The clan mothers had a pivotal role in all governmental decisions, and the status of women was so revered that rape was virtually unknown. By all standards, the Haudenosaunee were a remarkable civilization. Situated between the English and French colonial rivals for North America, they were a powerful buffer that each side sought to ingratiate with trade goods, weapons, and money. In the year of Ganiodaiio's birth, there was little to suggest that an apocalypse was soon to fall on his people.

But then came the Seven Years' War. From 1756 to 1763, France and Great Britain were locked into the first truly global war. The Haudenosaunee Confederacy was courted by each side as the fighting in North America between New France and the English colonies intensified. The Haudenosaunee supported the British but were left out of the Treaty of Paris in 1763 that ended the conflict. The French departed and the English took over what is now Canada. Without realizing it, the Haudenosaunee had lost their place as a buffer between two competing European powers and left themselves open to attack by a new force, the American settlers.

The Revolutionary War was the beginning of the Haudenosaunee apocalypse. As it began in 1776 the Haudenosaunee sought to remain neutral, but pro-British Mohawks and Onondagas raided nearby American settlements and the war came on them in a vengeance of retaliation. American armies in 1779 systematically burned villages, destroyed crops, massacred men, women, and children, and mutilated corpses to sow a sense of terror.

It is into this horrific context that we must situate the prophetic mission of Ganiodaiio. Under the terms of the Treaty of Big Tree in 1797, the Senecas gave up 95 percent of their territory to the American settlers. The situation among the other nations of the old Confederacy was just as bad. Haudenosaunee society bent under enormous pressure. Hunger and disease swept over the land. Alcoholism became endemic. A sense of political, economic, and spiritual collapse overwhelmed what had once been a model community. As the American Revolution signaled the birth of a new nation, it signaled the death of an old one.

— • —

Just as this physical apocalypse was beginning for the Haudenosaunee, their spiritual apocalypse as revelation was beginning as well. On June 15, 1799, a runner came to the home of the village chief, Cornplanter, to tell him that his brother lay dying in his cabin. It was not unexpected news, for Ganiodaiio had been in bad health for years, largely due to his acute alcoholism. Now, it seemed, the end had come. Cornplanter rushed to the scene to find his nephew Blacksnake already there with other family members. Two Quakers who had been working on a nearby schoolhouse were also present to record the events that followed. The family told Cornplanter that they had been outside the cabin, cleaning beans for planting, when they heard Ganiodaiio suddenly shout out *Niio!*—"So be it!" Then the sick man had appeared at the doorway, pale and unsteady. He fell forward, caught in the arms of his daughter. Blacksnake felt for a pulse and checked his breathing, but there was none. The body was cool to the touch. It appeared that Ganiodaiio was dead.

Blacksnake, however, felt there was something strange occurring, because he could detect a warm spot at the center of the apparently lifeless body. The family waited and prayed. In half an hour the breathing returned, shallow but perceptible. Then the pulse returned. The "warm spot" seemed to spread throughout the body. Then suddenly Ganiodaiio opened his eyes and began to speak. What he had to say changed Haudenosaunee history.

Ganiodaiio spontaneously recited an apocalyptic vision. He said that he had been lying on his sickbed when he heard his name being called. He struggled to his feet and walked to the door. There stood three middle-aged men, dressed in ceremonial clothes, with red paint dotted on their faces. They carried bows and arrows in one hand and huckleberry bushes in the other. They told Ganiodaiio that they were messengers from the Creator, sent to tell him a divine truth he must share with his people. This holy message was contained in only four words: four evil practices that upset the Creator and were destroying the nation.

Ganiodaiio told his brother to gather the people so they could hear for themselves what their Creator had to say.

This was during the Strawberry Festival, a major event for the Seneca people, so the community was easily gathered to hear what Ganiodaiio had to share. He told them the four evil words were *whiskey, witchcraft, charms,* and *abortion.* Essentially these words pointed to behaviors that were contrary to the will of the Creator. People were abusing alcohol, which was destroying families. In their hopelessness they were turning to the practitioners of dark magic to get what they needed. They were using magic charms to try to generate love rather than living in the love of the Creator. And finally, they were guilty of bad medicine, including medicine that could abort the birth of children. All these evil practices were happening because the nation had lost its way. The apocalypse of their social collapse could only be reversed by a spiritual reawakening that began within the heart of each individual. To effect this change, the people must become aware of their own faults and accept their personal responsibility. Ganiodaiio said that this process of accountability began in a new spiritual practice for the Haudenosaunee: confession.

People who were moderate sinners could confess to Ganiodaiio privately. People who were fairly innocent of these four bad behaviors could confess at public worship. And those who were guilty of evil acts should confess to the

Creator privately and seek amendment of life. Following
the presentation of this first vision and its requirements,
the Quaker scribes recorded that they "felt the love of God
flowing powerfully amongst us."

In the days following this first announcement of his
sacred mission, Ganiodaiio told his brother not to be
alarmed if he seemed to die again. The three messengers
from heaven had told him that there was a fourth messenger who would soon make his appearance. On the night of
August 7 it came to pass as Ganiodaiio had explained. The
prophet fell into a coma, again with no perceptible heartbeat or breathing, which lasted seven hours. On awakening
from this trance-like state, Ganiodaiio recounted that he
had been visited by the fourth messenger. This vision was
recorded by one of the visiting Quakers, Henry Simmons.

Dressed in sky-blue clothes, the fourth messenger took
Ganiodaiio on a journey over the Milky Way. He guided
the prophet in a way that echoes Dante's epic poem *The
Inferno*: a guided tour through an otherworldly landscape,
with a series of scenes that the prophet is asked to com-
ment on. For example, the fourth messenger showed the
prophet a church with a spire and a path leading in, but no
door or window. Inside they heard wailing and moaning.
The vision was interpreted as illustrating what happens
to Native people when they are confined to Christianity.
They saw two great drops of an unknown liquid, one red

and one yellow, suspended in the sky. These were visual images for impending disasters: potential pandemics that would bring death over the earth, the very thing Ganiodaiio must prevent through his teachings. These teachings were collected into a single text, memorized by his followers, and later written down, called the Gaiwiio, the "Good Message" (also the "Good Way" or the "Good Word").

Then, in an extraordinary scene, Ganiodaiio met Jesus, still bearing the marks of his crucifixion. Jesus asked how the Seneca people are doing in receiving the new teachings of the Gaiwiio. The prophet replied that he thought about half the people believed him. Jesus said this is better than he had done with his own people and encouraged Ganiodaiio to tell the Indigenous people not to follow the ways of the white man or they would become lost. The vision concluded with a truly Dante-like visit to hell: the house of the Punisher, where a shapeshifter spirit rules over those who took the wrong path. Like the writer of the book of Revelation, Ganiodaiio saw a mystical tableau of both the joys of the afterlife and its potential horrors.

On returning from this epic spiritual journey, Ganiodaiio led the people in a new dance, the Worship Dance, which would hold the physical apocalypse at bay. It was shortly after this revelation that Ganiodaiio received the blessing of his most important convert, his half-sister, Gayantgogwus, a clan-mother and a great medicine woman. Not

unlike Muhammad in the early period of the establish-
ment of Islam, it was the support of family members that
grounded the new faith and spread confidence in the Gaiwiio, the Good Way.

On February 5, 1800, the prophet had a third vision
that instructed him to prepare the way of Gaiwiio not only
through song and dance but in a transcribed version. The
focus of this third vision was salvation: personal responsibility and self-awareness rooted in the practice of the
ancient traditions of the Haudenosaunee people. The recitation of the Good Way was fixed on certain times each
year, creating a sacred calendar. These precepts of the new
faith were memorized by people from different villages.
Cornplanter and Ganiodaiio undertook teaching missions
to other Haudenosaunee villages. The new religion spread
rapidly, filling the vacuum of hope left by the destruction
of the old Confederacy.

— • —

In the late winter of 1802, Ganiodaiio was ready to take
his apocalyptic vision as high as it could reach. He went to
Washington, DC, to meet with the president of the United
States, Thomas Jefferson. Accompanied by some of his
followers, he had a meeting with Jefferson and explained
his mission:

The Great Spirit has appointed four Angels and appointed me the fifth to direct our people on Earth. He directed me to begin with my own people first and that is why I have been so long in coming to my white Brother. I am very much troubled that my Brothers and my white Brothers have gone astray. I have now come forward to make us love one another again with your assistance.

Ganiodaiio sought to convert Thomas Jefferson to an Indigenous vision of equality between the Native people and the American settlers. He failed to do so, but he was very successful in winning the minds and hearts of his own people. The Haudenosaunee embraced his teachings.

For fifteen years Ganiodaiio and his followers developed a religious community among the Haudenosaunee. They kept the sacred calendar, reciting the precepts of the Good Way at the appointed times. They performed the songs and dances integral to worship in the new faith. By 1815 Ganiodaiio was an aging prophet with a youthful following. In one of his final visions, he spoke of leaving his new religion with his people:

The day was bright when I went into the planted field and alone I wandered in the planted field and it was the time of the second hoeing. Suddenly a damsel appeared and threw her arms about my neck and as she clasped me she spoke saying, "When you leave this earth for the new world above, it is our wish to follow you." I looked for the damsel but saw only the long leaves of corn twining around my shoulders. And then I understood it was the spirit of the corn who had spoken, she the sustainer of life. So I replied, "O spirit of the corn, follow not me but abide still upon the earth and be strong and be faithful to your purpose. Ever endure and do not fail the children of women. It is not time for you to follow, for the Gaiwiio is only in its beginning."

Ganiodaiio died in 1815 on a teaching mission to the Onondaga Reservation. As was his custom, he had walked the seventy-five miles from his home to the land of the Onondagas with a few followers. Once there, he began to feel sick and was given a place to rest in a local home. People in great numbers gathered outside, praying and singing in the Gaiwiio tradition. Although growing weaker, Ganiodaiio came out of the house to speak to them. It was his final sermon.

I will soon go to my new home. Soon I will step into the new world for there is a plain pathway before me leading there. Whoever follows my teachings will follow in my footsteps and I will look back upon them with outstretched arms inviting them into the new world of our Creator. Alas, I fear that a pall of smoke will obscure the eyes of many from the truth of Gaiwiio but I pray that when I am gone that all may do what I have taught.

Today the religion of Ganiodaiio is still practiced among the Haudenosaunee. The Code of Handsome Lake—the Gaiwiio—is still recited at the proper times in the Longhouse, the focal point for woodland cultures across North America as a place of sacred community gatherings. The Longhouse tradition is sustained by the Good Way. It is a testimony to how well the prophet met the apocalyptic challenge faced by his people. One historian has written, using the translation of the prophet's name,

> Handsome Lake kept alive many truly authentic aspects of Haudenosaunee culture that were threatened with extinction by a juggernaut of coerced assimilation. While some aspects of his teachings occasioned controversy and strife, the continued observance of the great religious festivals, the survival of clan organization, the communal ethic, and persistence of a distinctive Iroquoian sense of identity all reflect the influence of Handsome Lake.

Handsome Lake, Ganiodaiio, helped his people survive the apocalyptic events of his time. His teachings helped to preserve their ancient traditions. They kept the culture together. The Gaiwiio became a catalyst for a sober, ethical, and spiritual community to coalesce around faith. It worked and continues to work for many Haudenosaunee people.

But what does it have to offer those of us outside the Longhouse? What lessons can we learn from the message of Ganiodaiio?

— • —

Since answering that question will be the process we will use for all of the four prophets in this book, let us be clear from the outset that our goal is not to try to appropriate the Gaiwiio or remove it from its context in traditional Haudenosaunee culture. Given the constraints of our study, we cannot do justice to the whole of Ganiodaiio's experience or teaching. We can only sketch the historical reality he faced and gather a few key insights into the nature of his response. It is a brief glimpse into the depth of the Good Way, but it is enough to give us a foothold in the apocalyptic process. It allows us to ask, What can we learn from the Gaiwiio? How can Ganiodaiio's message speak to us in our own apocalyptic moment in history?

My reply may surprise you. In giving it, I could try to conform to a politically correct image of a Native American mystic. Ironically, in the apocalyptic culture in which we now live, that happens more often than not. Native American spirituality is appropriated into a reassuring mixture of New Age prophecies and postcolonial sentimentality. We could do that with Ganiodaiio—or with any other of the prophets we will examine in this book. But any reassurance or insight that such an exercise would provide would be shallow and short-lived. Romantic notions of a guru of the forest would be a frail response to the looming apocalypse that many of us fear is slowly rising up before us.

If this book is to have value, it must be able to take the spiritual message of the Native American prophets, with both their strengths and shortcomings, and apply them directly to our own situation without any sugar coating.

For example, as a Native American, I am troubled by the imagery in the Gaiwiio that paints a picture of hell. In the Gaiwiio, the scenes in the house of the Punisher are very reminiscent of the worst Puritan expectations of what will happen to unrepentant sinners. While most traditional spirituality in North America before the coming of the Europeans included an expectation of the afterlife, they did not have the graphic depictions of a hell as you find in the Gaiwiio. You will not find that kind of apocalyptic vision because the act on which it is predicated, sin, is not present in the Indigenous tradition. Sin, as understood in Judaism, Christianity, and Islam, for example, is not foundational in Native America. Wrongdoing was certainly acknowledged, but long lists of sinful behavior and graphic illustrations of divine punishment are absent.

So why do we find it in the Good Way?

A quick answer would be cultural borrowing. Remember the Quakers who were at Ganiodaiio's first vision? The presence of white Christian missionaries from many denominations in the Seneca nation is well documented, as is the contact the Haudenosaunee had with neighboring white settlements. Even if a Seneca person was completely traditional in their lifestyle and avoided contact with white people as much as possible, we would be hard pressed to say that they would have no knowledge of the nature of religious beliefs of the other culture. Certainly it would have been in Ganiodaiio's experience, given that his vision specifically identifies Jesus and the Christian church.

Could Ganiodaiio have borrowed images from his white neighbors? The answer has to be yes, even if we respect the integrity of the prophet by saying this could have happened subconsciously. Ancient Israel borrowed from Mesopotamia. Christianity borrowed from Judaism. Islam borrowed from both. Naming the reality is not denigrating the faith but keeping it in the apocalyptic process of which we are all a part. Faced with an apocalyptic event that was impacting his people like a tsunami, it is easy to imagine that Ganiodaiio, like his contemporaries, would have many spiritual images, hopes, and fears running through his mind as he struggled to find a response that would be powerful enough to change their suffering.

As an alcoholic, Ganiodaiio also carried a heavy burden of guilt. The accounts of his life recorded at the time all bear witness to that fact. He was a person tormented by a behavior he could not seem to control. He was aware, as any twelve-step program will validate, that he had done things in his drunkenness that he deeply regretted. Lying on what he imagined to be his deathbed, he may have been coming to terms with his actions and dreading the consequences. The echo of the white concept of sin may have entered into his vision not as an intentional borrowing but as a result of his own personal struggle.

Whatever the source or reason, Ganiodaiio's introduction of sin and of hell into the Haudenosaunee religious vocabulary shifted the equation of their traditional teachings. In this way, Ganiodaiio was not just a champion of the old tradition but a reformer—an agent of change. As the Buddha believed he was bringing a message of reform to Hinduism and Jesus was a reformer of Judaism, so Ganiodaiio proclaimed a reform of Haudenosaunee religion. Like all reformers, he kept some things and abandoned others. And, like all reformers, he was both lauded and despised for doing so.

During his lifetime he was accused of syncretism. His white critics vilified him for perverting Christianity, and his Haudenosaunee critics criticized him for violating the sacred tradition of the Great Law of Peace. He stood in the midst of this controversy and continued to insist that his path could not only save his people from the apocalyptic end of Native American culture but actually prevent an even greater apocalypse: a possible lethal pandemic, envisioned in the two giant drops of liquid hanging over humanity like a sword of Damocles. Extreme situations call for extreme responses: this may have been the tradeoff in the mind of the prophet that opened the door to discussions of sin and hell.

Why this novel and disturbing teaching about sin is there—either as the absolute revelation of a truth from the Creator or as an internalized projection of the person Cornplanter described at the beginning of this chapter— we may never know. But the fact is it is there: a concept of sin injected into traditional Native American spirituality. Does that invalidate the message of Ganiodaiio? If we were looking for the politically correct Native American image, our answer would be yes. We would be disappointed that Ganiodaiio was not the Hollywood version of the wise old medicine man and move on to find someone else. But from my vantage point as a Native American elder, I would say no: we do not ignore Ganiodaiio simply because he preached hellfire and brimstone. So have many other prophets of all faiths. I say we look deeper. Look through the apocalyptic process to see what the prophet's choices reveal to us on an even deeper level.

Ganiodaiio may not be the ideal image of the Native American prophet, but he is worthy of our respect and attention, if for no other reason than because his prophecy worked. Ganiodaiio did help to save his people. He succeeded in preserving the very traditions he was reforming. He kept the Longhouse intact, and he maintained the ancient clan system. He institutionalized the songs and dances of his culture. When we survey the tragic landscape of the American Apocalypse—the colonization of North America by European settlers—as it decimated so many Native American cultures, one high and hopeful point still stands out. The Haudenosaunee are not gone and forgotten, but still very present in their Longhouse tradition. And much of the credit goes to the influence of Ganiodaiio and his Gaiwiio.

— • —

So what do those of us living in this time and place learn from the Gaiwiio? Is our only lesson the one of sin and hell? That would not provide much comfort. Not only would it be a disappointing image of the Native American prophet; it would also reaffirm the proclamation of this same teaching in fundamentalist communities of all types and persuasions. Doom and gloom, hellfire and retribution, sin and blame: we are already awash in those messages. In fact, they are a big part of the apocalyptic process that got us here in the first place. If we take the Gaiwiio at face value, it becomes just a small part of a much larger judgmental narrative.

But if we ask about its revelation, it becomes a far more expansive and hopeful vision of how we can cope with the critical change of apocalypse. The apocalyptic twist Ganiodaiio introduces to traditional Native theology is more than just the addition of sin and hell. Yes, that is a novel and perhaps contentious element. But from the Native perspective, something even deeper is revealed in his teaching: the shift from thinking in the "we" to thinking in the "me."

Like all North American Indigenous cultures, the traditional Haudenosaunee were a communal society. Their Great Law of Peace formalized that understanding. There was no concept of private ownership of the land, a spiritual principle that the Gaiwiio affirms. The society was a tightly woven community of kinship. Children were raised to think of others first, the greatest common good, rather than their own desires or needs. Food gathered from the harvest or the hunt was shared. The scales of authority and governance were carefully calibrated so no single person could have more influence than another. The mindset of the individual was turned toward considering the "we" before thinking of the "me." It is, therefore, no surprise that when Karl Marx and Friedrich Engels were searching for an example of early communism in human history they looked directly at the culture of the Haudenosaunee.

Understanding the nature of this deeply communal culture is important because it underscores what a radical prophet Ganiodaiio really was. He not only introduced ideas of sin and damnation into the spirituality of his people; he turned their thinking about the spiritual role of the individual upside down. Where traditional Haudenosaunee culture had stressed the primacy of the collective, Ganiodaiio focused squarely on the individual. Each individual must be accountable for their own actions. The balance of the apocalypse rested on their personal choices.

The fulcrum for Ganiodaiio's teaching can be identified in another spiritual practice he introduced: confession. The Haudenosaunee had never practiced confession because there was no religious code of behavior in which to ground it. They had the ethical obligations and relationships of the communal society, but there was no doctrine of sin to require confession. Confession, as stipulated in the Gaiwiio, was something new, something radical to Haudenosaunee tradition. And as problematic as it may seem to some of us who are outside the Longhouse, the reversal of the poles between "me" and "we" seemed to work. It stabilized the community. It created a great reduction in the level of alcohol abuse among the people. It united the nation in a revitalization of the old values that had always sustained Haudenosaunee society, but with a new emphasis on personal responsibility.

Essentially, Ganiodaiio took a radical prophetic action, one designed to invert the nature of his culture. He shifted their spiritual focus from the communal collapse they saw all around them. He turned their gaze from the breakdown of the many to the redemption of the individual. He replaced their internal grief with hope for positive change. Through confession, either public or private, he gave them a path back to wholeness. It may be argued that his own struggles with alcoholism informed his wisdom. He understood that the Haudenosaunee needed a recovery model that worked on the personal level, since they had hit bottom in their apocalyptic fall. As jarring as it was, this insistence on individual confession released the guilt, shame, and sorrow of his people. He gave them a way out of despair and a path to recovery.

In fact, the Gaiwiio continues to this day not only as a religion but as the basis for an alcohol treatment process among Indigenous people. In *The Path of Handsome Lake: A Model of Recovery for Native People*, Dr. Alf H. Walle offers this clear summary of Ganiodaiio's achievement:

Handsome Lake, responding to cultural and economic stress facing his people 200 years ago, forged a sophisticated strategy of cultural renewal by which people could relieve the pain of cultural decline while simultaneously dealing with their own dysfunction in forceful and concrete ways. Largely through Handsome Lake's efforts, the Iroquois people were able to stem their dysfunctional response to the pressures they faced and embark on a powerful cultural renaissance. The three-prong approach that Handsome Lake recommended includes (1) a re-embrace of the people's cultural traditions, (2) an adjustment of the culture so that it could successfully cope with the contemporary situation that people faced, and (3) overcoming dysfunctional patterns of behavior coupled with a penance for past misdeeds.

The apocalyptic revelation that Ganiodaiio offers to us today is contained in that simple phrase: "an adjustment of the culture." The prophet adjusted Haudenosaunee culture by turning its cultural vision upside down. He balanced the communal with the individual, and by so doing, released a healing power among his people.

If there is a lesson to be learned from the Gaiwiio, a revelation that can offer us hope for the future, it is in this exact apocalyptic process: to turn our own culture upside down.

Contemporary American society is the reverse of traditional Native American culture. Whereas Native communities value the group, the dominant society values the individual. In fact, it considers rugged individualism to be a virtue. It looks up to the "self-made" success story. It honors the person who can acquire more than anyone else. It likes heroes who can go it alone and role models who make their own rules. It disparages collective action as a herd mentality and prefers individuals with the right to do as they choose. For millions of people, individuality has evolved into individualism: a cult of personality in which they are the personality.

The consequences of this individualistic society should be apparent as we survey the apocalyptic situation in which we find ourselves. Many of our most persistent problems have to do with greed, with the desire of some individuals to have more than others. Arrogance fuels many of our deepest social issues. A sense of entitlement and privilege haunts us as we try to create a cohesive society. We struggle to make any concerted effort to cope with environmental change because any significant response would impact our individual lifestyles. It would require sacrifice, and most of us would prefer for someone else to make that sacrifice. We are, therefore, the ultimate "me" society. Even in the face of a common apocalyptic danger, we will not come together. Our attachment to individualism has blunted our ability to confront racism, immigration, education reform, medical care, and even the ability to vote. In other words, when called on to face the apocalyptic challenges before us, we fail to make a unified response; instead, we fragment into ever smaller units of privilege.

The prophecy of Ganiodaiio shows us what we have to do: make "an adjustment of the culture." We will have to challenge some of the bedrock assumptions of our society and confront individualism head on. When we do, we must be prepared for an outpouring of denial, objections, threats, and conflict. To question individualism is to question an addiction of the dominant society, the mythic ground on which so much of our shared colonial history is centered. Rugged individualism came over on the *Mayflower*. It rode with the 7th Cavalry, as we will see later in this book. It built skyscrapers and invented the Bomb. It is not to be trifled with. But it can be changed.

Like Ganiodaiio, we will be suggesting a radical reform to a battered community. We will be asking people to accept a counterintuitive idea. We will be asking them to try on a realignment of their thinking. It will be changing old habits while creating a new groove in the public psyche of our generation. But it has to be done. Because until we do make an adjustment of major proportions, we are never going to mitigate the apocalypse we are facing. In fact, we will be helping it grow stronger.

The people who accepted the Gaiwiio did so because they believed their radical situation demanded a radical response. They were facing a massive military invasion, widespread disease, and the social collapse of a centuries-old civilization. Shifting from a cultural vision of the "we" to the "me" was a risk—a leap of faith—but they were willing to do it to stave off the apocalypse that was consuming them. They trusted their spiritual instincts, and they were right. They did push back the apocalypse of their time and place. They experienced a renewal. They changed the equation of their history.

We can do the same thing. All we have to do is reverse the equation. We need to go in the opposite direction of the Haudenosaunee. We need to shift from the "me" to the "we." Admittedly, that will not be an easy thing to do. When we face a crisis that requires unified action, many people refuse to cooperate, even if to do so is in their own best interests, because they want to hold onto their individual prerogatives. In the midst of an apocalyptic challenge, they turn away from creating a shared solution to focus on how change is impacting them personally. Personal privilege outweighs community survival. In a health-care crisis, for example, the mentality of rugged individualism becomes a rallying cry against cooperation. People reject inoculations against disease, even if by doing so they make the spread of the disease worse.

That mentality does not bode well for our future. If Ganiodaiio's drops of liquid ever fall to earth, that kind of individualistic mindset will prove lethal.

— • —

So how can we make a cultural adjustment before it is too late? One approach is right in front of us: teach American history. Not colonial history, but the Indigenous history of the Americas. For generations the youth of North America have been raised with a very narrow version of the history that shaped their culture. They have seen it through the keyhole of individualism. We can show it to them in the wide panorama of scores of Native American nations who collectively embody a powerful vision of community.

A truly Indigenous history of America offers a case study in how communities like the Haudenosaunee functioned before the colonial invasion. These are not perfect societies, but they are practical societies. They worked. They worked as cooperative communities where the rights and needs of the individual were integrated with the hopes and needs of the whole people. While it is true that Native American nations were so communal that Europeans like Marx and Engels looked at them as prototypes for a utopian civilization, it is also true that they were societies made up of enormously individualistic citizens.

Native American people lived in highly communal ways, but individual Native citizens lived a very libertarian existence. They were free to go where they wanted, when they wanted, and how they wanted. They had their own personal vision of the sacred. They painted those visions on the outside of their homes to announce their unique vision to others in their community. As we will see in the next chapter, they could not be coerced into going to war, even in the face of a foreign invasion. And their sense of personal liberty was not reserved just for male members of the community. A Native American woman of the eighteenth century had far more individual rights than her European counterpart. She could vote, hold her own land, and divorce her husband. Consequently, while Native American nations operated on a highly communal principle, they also maintained a highly individualistic society.

The difference is between individuality and individualism. The Indigenous history of the Americas reveals that difference. As a Native American, I have often seen how quickly conversations about collective solutions to problems are shouted down in our society. Take health care, for example. Something as foundational to any culture as the ability of its inhabitants to receive quality health care can be derailed by a single word: *socialism*. That word is like a silver bullet. It can kill any dialogue on national health care in a second. It can do so because it conjures up images of a society where no one has individual rights but is forced to live like a robot controlled by a central authority. It is a mythic word made potent by the power of fear. An accurate study of the historical experience of Indigenous nations could help to demystify that fear. It could do so by making an apocalyptic revelation: it is possible for people to cooperate without losing their civil liberties. A balance is possible. An equilibrium between the individual and the community can be created and maintained, just as it was in the Great Law of Peace.

Teaching our history from the ground up is one immediate step we can take on the path from the "me" to the "we." Sharing this information in all forms of media can be an effective method for opening minds and hearts to an apocalyptic revelation, a positive rediscovery of our shared past in terms that can be both inspiring and healing. The history of Native American nations can counterbalance the story of conquest, occupation, and oppression that still shapes the dominant worldview. It will take a concerted effort to make this shift in perspective, but it is possible. It is grounded in the reality of our shared American experience. Individualism, with its macho mentality and its fear-based reactions, can be challenged and replaced. The facts can speak for themselves. The comparisons can be disclosed. The apocalyptic process can reveal an alternative: a viable, practical, effective alternative. And the more that people are exposed to this alternative, the more they will opt for a choice that allows maximum freedom to the individual while preserving a united front.

We will discuss some of this history in the next chapter, when we see how individuality and apocalypse played out in America before the War of 1812. But for now, let us focus on what Ganiodaiio has shown us. While we may question his theology of sin and hell—which is not much different from the theology expounded in faith communities across mainstream America today—we can see how a shift in the balance of perception helped release a powerful realignment in the apocalyptic equation of his time. His emphasis on personal responsibility, and on confession and reconciliation, turned his followers from despair to hope. His cultural adjustment from the "we" to the "me" had a dramatic result: a quantifiable result as the levels of dysfunctional behavior dropped and the cohesion of the community increased. His Gaiwiio set in motion what one observer called a "renaissance" among the Haudenosaunee people.

The key was preserving the traditional spiritual teaching and practice of the Haudenosaunee, but doing so in a new context of personal accountability. Rather than watch their ancient culture crumble around them, the men and women who adopted the Good Way believed they could each make a difference. They took up the challenge of survival as their individual commitment. They carried out the songs and dances, the seasonal recitations of Gaiwiio, and the use of confession in order to push back the apocalypse that was overwhelming their community. And it worked. Native tradition stood up to European colonialism, at least spiritually, and the ancient history of the people continued into the next centuries.

If we are willing to do what the followers of Ganio-daiio did—if we are willing to turn our worldview upside down to bring balance to our behavior—we can meet the challenges of our apocalypse and preserve the values we cherish for the next generation. We can turn from individualism to individuality, preserve our personal liberties, and at the same time evolve into a functioning community. We can follow the lead of Indigenous societies that worked together for the common good, provided for the least of their citizens, and survived the American Apocalypse. It will require a new humility inspired by an old faith, but together we can do it if we are willing to restore balance and work together.

3

TENSKWATAWA

The House of the Stranger

He was divested of all his tinkling ornaments but a round gorget on his breast that fastened his garment. His dress was plain and decent, his countenance grave and solemn. His person was of a common size, rather slender and of no great appearance. All was silent for some time. He began to speak, and with his eyes closed continued his speech about half an hour in a very eloquent and emphatical manner. He sensibly spake by the power of God—his solemn voice, grave countenance, with every motion of his hand and gesture of his body, were expressive of a deep sense and solemn feeling of eternal things. . . . At every remarkable pause or sentence, a solemn assent sounded.

—Benjamin Young

THOMAS JEFFERSON HAD a plan. Looking at the map of the United States, which covered the eastern seaboard of North America from Maine to Georgia (Florida still belonging to Spain), he recognized that it bordered some of the best farmland in the world. Just over the Appalachian Mountains were vast territories that could be opened to white settlement. This fertile and profitable real estate could more than double the size of the young nation. It was a prize for the taking. All he had to do was keep an eye on the British in Canada and then deal with the current occupants of his vision of westward expansion: a patchwork quilt of scores of small Native American nations.

The Shawnee, Delawares, Wyandots, Miamis, Ottawas, Cherokees, and many more: the first step must be to dispossess them all of their land, but to do so in a cheaper way than armed conflict, if possible. What Jefferson needed was a scheme for bargain-basement colonialism.

In a letter of instruction for his new governor of the Northwest Territories (Ohio, Illinois, Indiana), William Henry Harrison, the president sketched out how he was going to make the Indians a deal they could not refuse:

We wish to draw the Indians to agriculture. . . . When they withdraw themselves to the culture of a small piece of land, they will perceive how useless to them are their extensive forests, and be willing to pare them off in exchange for necessaries for their farms and families. To promote this disposition to exchange lands . . . we shall push our trading houses and be glad to see them run up a debt because when these debts get beyond what the Indians can pay, they will become willing to lop them off by a cession of lands. . . . In this way our settlement will gradually circumscribe and approach the Indians, and they will either incorporate with us as citizens of the United States or remove beyond the Mississippi River. . . . Should any tribe be foolhardy enough to take up the hatchet, the seizing the whole country of that tribe and driving them across the Mississippi as the only condition of peace would be an example to others and a furtherance of our final consolidation.

Governor Harrison followed these instructions over the beginning years of the nineteenth century, and he also refined Jefferson's plan with some strategies of his own. He identified local village chiefs of small communities who would be willing to sign treaties if they were promised annuities, both cash and goods, that would be paid to them on a regular basis. They were expected to share some of this bounty with their people, but how and if that happened was entirely up to them. There were no checks or balances. But there was a great deal of whiskey, which figured prominently at all treaty negotiations.

By using this methodology, along with Jefferson's debt scheme, Harrison was able to claim huge swaths of land traditionally occupied by Native American nations. In 1803, for example, under the Treaty of Fort Wayne he obtained almost the entire area of what is now Illinois. A year later, in 1804, he swindled the Sauk and Foxes people out of 51 million acres. The cost to the United States was as little as a penny an acre.

The apocalypse that Native nations between the Appalachians and the Mississippi faced from the end of the American Revolution until the end of the War of 1812 was a carefully orchestrated one. It moved according to the Jeffersonian model: to manipulate a handful of collaborators to cede land, whether it was theirs or not, through the use of alcohol and bribes; to force individual Native people into debt to the company store, so their land could be seized in payment; and to physically attack any who resisted and force them out of the United States, so their land would be taken by right of conquest and so their peers would be cowed into submission. It was a system worthy of the mafia, and it worked over and over again as the Long Knives—the common name among these Native nations for the settlers—continued to carve up Native sovereignty bit by bit.

Not all Native leaders were corruptible, of course. But only a handful of accomplices were needed to get signatures on treaties so maps could be drawn that squeezed Native nations into ever smaller amounts of their own territory. Once those maps had been drawn, once the land was surveyed, then Native people could be attacked for stepping over the line, even if it was on land that had been theirs for generations. To add to the intimidation, white settlers who killed Native Americans for crossing the line were never convicted of murder, while Native Americans who killed white settlers were executed.

Legitimate Native leaders recognized this colonial system for what it was and fought back. As early as 1763 the Ottawa chief Pontiac had been inspired by a Native prophet, Neolin, to take up arms against the land-hungry settlers, and he was able to stop them in their tracks. At least for a while. Pontiac became a folk hero for Native Americans and a cautionary tale for white colonizers. The specter of a visionary prophet lifting up an incorruptible leader was a powerful one because it had actually happened.

Pontiac's name still struck fear into hearts like Governor William Henry Harrison's, and it still kept hope alive among the increasingly desperate Indigenous communities in what is now Ohio, Kentucky, Illinois, Michigan, and Indiana. Neolin had a vision of liberation for Native people that had swept through the Great Lakes area, and Pontiac had taken that vision and tried to make it real. Apocalyptic pressure creates apocalyptic leaders. The apocalyptic process begins when actual events become an apocalyptic disaster, and the only recourse is an apocalyptic revelation that can show people a way out.

A decade after Pontiac and Neolin, the machinery of American expansion was grinding away after the British had been driven out. The apocalyptic situation was ripe for another vision.

— • —

The man who was to supply that vision was born in 1775 in a Shawnee village called Old Piqua on the Mad River in western Ohio. His birth was far from being heralded by heavenly signs or wonders. In fact, his birth was considered an evil omen, because he was one of triplets. Among his people, the Shawnee, multiple births were thought of as bad luck. In this case, one of the triplets, a little girl, had died, which meant she took the bad with her. But the life of one brother, Lalawethika, would not be much easier.

As a child, Lalawethika became blind in one eye after an accident with a metal-tipped arrow. He lost his father in one of the endless border conflicts with American settlers, the Battle of Point Pleasant. His mother eventually left her children with relatives as she moved farther west to escape the violence.

As a young man, Lalawethika was not an accomplished hunter or warrior. In fact, he was just the opposite. Among his own people he was called "Big Mouth" because he overcompensated for his shortcomings with braggadocio. Not being able to excel in other ways, Lalawethika tried to become a medicine man, a role his people needed badly to cope with the pandemics like smallpox that ravaged their families. He sought training as an apprentice under a recognized spiritual teacher, Penagasha, but unfortunately his skill was lacking in this vocation as well.

Eventually, his many failures brought Lalawethika to seek comfort in drinking, and he became a notorious alcoholic in his community. In this time, as part of the colonial strategy of the United States, whiskey and rum were easily accessible for Native Americans. It was what helped them run up deep debts from American traders. So Lalawethika had no trouble finding his drug of choice. His people, however, shunned him or ignored him. He married, but he lived a marginal existence in a world where his people were already marginal enough.

His story might have ended there—just another anonymous Indian who succumbed to alcohol—when something strange happened. In 1805, as Lalawethika was sitting by the fire in his lodge, he reached out to find a brand to light his long-stem pipe. Suddenly his body went rigid, and he dropped the brand and fell over as if dead. His wife called neighbors, and they rushed in to discover his body already rigid. There was no breathing or pulse. Assuming he had died from his excessive drinking, they prepared his body for burial: washing and clothing him in his best attire, painting his face, and laying out his body for his family to pray over before the burial. His grave was dug.

Twenty-four hours later, just as the family was gathered to take the lifeless body to the gravesite, Lalawethika opened his eyes. As his startled relatives recoiled in shock and fear, he began to speak to them. The apocalyptic revelation of the Prophet, as he came to be known, had begun.

It is interesting to note how often apocalyptic revelations, recounted by mystics and prophets around the world, contain the same basic elements. For example, there are often spirit guides—angelic figures that appear and take the "dead" person on a journey. These messengers are an integral part of the revelation, as they show the mortal human being heavenly or hellish visions. They interpret these images and explain the prophet's impending mission. So it was with Lalawethika.

In a very similar experience to the one recounted by Ganiodaiio, Lalawethika reported that two messengers from God—called the Master of Life in Shawnee culture—took him to heaven. He was not allowed to enter heaven, but he could see it and it was wonderful. It fulfilled the most ancient promise to the Shawnee: that they were the first of the human beings to be created and the chosen ones, along with all other Indigenous people. They were to inherit a land full of clear water teeming with fish, herds of animals, and broad fields of corn. It was a paradise of beauty and plenty.

As we shall see later, this vision of a peaceful afterlife was central to the Native American prophetic encounter. All four prophets we will consider had a nearly identical image of the heaven they saw in their mystic journey. It was a Native American dream-like reality, a return to the lifestyle of Native people before the coming of the Europeans. In fact, the question of a European presence in the vision of the prophets becomes a critical issue. Did the prophets see any white people in the afterlife? As we shall see, this question becomes a tipping point for the spiritual relationship between the Indigenous people and their oppressors.

And yet, like many apocalyptic revelations, there was a flip side to the apocalyptic coin. There was another road the messengers showed him, one that did not lead to heaven but to hell. It was a scene worthy of the Dutch artist Hieronymus Bosch. Sinful people were ushered into a large lodge, where a fire was burning continuously. There they suffered punishment for their bad behavior. Unrepentant drunkards, for example, were forced to drink molten lead until flames came out of their noses and ears. This contrast between eternal joy and sorrow was made explicit and graphic by Lalawethika as he recounted his vision to his family, still dressed in his burial clothes with his face painted for death. When he finished speaking, he collapsed into weeping and trembling.

So sincere was his message that many who gathered around him that day became his first converts. Most important among them was one family member in particular: his older brother by seven years, Tecumseh.

— • —

Hollywood casting could not find another man better suited to be the "Pontiac" to Lalawethika's "Neolin" than Tecumseh. The brothers could not have been more different. Tecumseh was tall, handsome, accomplished, and noble. He was considered the best hunter among all the Shawnees and their neighboring nations. He was a fearless warrior, and yet he was renowned for showing mercy to prisoners and kindness to women and children. He was an astute politician and such a persuasive speaker that even his adversaries respected him. When Tecumseh said he believed his brother's vision to be true, many other hearts followed him. They let go of the person of Lalawethika, the alcoholic braggart, and embraced Tecumseh's brother by a new name, a prophetic name: Tenskwatawa, the Open Door.

Over the following months Tenskwatawa had more visitations and revelations. He began his teaching in earnest, outlining the new apocalyptic faith of his people. As recorded by both Native American and white listeners, like three Shaker men who traveled to hear him preach, Tenskwatawa's gospel emerged from the ancient spirituality of his ancestors but insisted on the reform of some of these historic practices. He said that while it was true that the Master of Life had first created the Native people and blessed them, it was also true that they had fallen short in their behavior and beliefs. The reliance on medicine bundles, for example, was misplaced because these bundles were not able to stop the even more powerful medicine of the white colonizers. The Shawnee, and all converts to the new faith, needed new dances and new prayers to combat the evil that was before them. Not all settlers were evil, but the system they represented was evil and the Maker of Life would eventually destroy that kind of oppression. There would be an apocalyptic overturning of cultures, with the white society losing its control and Native people being restored to freedom. To help that happen, he said, believers in the new faith must stay away from white people. They should not wear white clothing or use white technology but return to the styles and practices of their ancestors.

Tenskwatawa's visions went on to reveal the ethical and moral precepts that should shape a believer's life. No more war or killing between Native nations. Truth telling in all negotiations. Respect for all women. Reverence for the earth and all her creatures. Above all, a deep communal sense of life and creation. Private ownership of land was to be repudiated. No more land was to be ceded or sold. Native people should hold all things in common and share whatever they had with one another. Generosity was to be a cornerstone of the new faith as it restored ancient values and traditions.

In this way Tenskwatawa's message was both an affirmation of traditional Native American virtues and a reform of those traditions to meet the new challenges of American perfidy. Tenskwatawa taught that Americans were created by a different god from Native people. This malevolent spirit had shaped white people from the foam of the great ocean, where an enormous and apocalyptic crab hid beneath the waves to carry out its evil designs. Only by living in love with one another, living in the old ways, could Native people drive back the land-hungry Americans and restore peace to the world.

Not since the days of Pontiac and Neolin had such a reformation been so profoundly preached and so widely accepted. Within a year, word about the new prophet was spreading from Florida to the Great Lakes.

Tenskwatawa's apocalyptic vision was attracting scores of followers from many Native nations throughout the border regions with the United States. Delawares, Kickapoos, Miamis, Ottawas, Wyandots: the nations living beside the Shawnee were open to Tenskwatawa's message because they had firsthand experience with the oppression the Prophet described. Other nations, such as the Ojibwe and Dakota, who were still at a distance from the main conflict, were interested in the Prophet's teaching, as they hoped to reverse the tide before it reached them. While many prominent figures opposed Tenskwatawa's gospel, especially those chiefs who he accused of taking bribes to sell their birthright, the flow of new believers increased daily. In turn, Tenskwatawa sent out his own missionaries to teach people the message of Native renewal and instruct them in the new dances of his faith. These missionaries "baptized" converts through a ritual known as "shaking hands with the prophet"; they would pass a rosary of beans touched by the Prophet through their hands as a sign of accepting his vision as their own.

— • —

It was during this time of burgeoning growth that the territorial governor, the Prophet's nemesis, William Henry Harrison, sought to discredit him once and for all. "If he is really a prophet," Harrison wrote in an open letter to Native people, "ask him to cause the sun to stand still—the moon to alter its course—the rivers to cease to flow—or the dead to rise from their graves. If he does these things then believe that he has been sent from God."

Much to Harrison's surprise, Tenskwatawa accepted his challenge. He invited all his followers to gather at a small village in June of that year so they could see the miracle for themselves. The faithful gathered on that date, and while the Prophet remained within his lodge, they suddenly witnessed a "black sun": a total eclipse. Just at the darkest moment of the eclipse the Prophet emerged, to the acclaim of his believers.

What actually happened that day—whether it was an apocalyptic sign or just a natural event—is open to interpretation, but the fact remains that the Prophet stole his accuser's thunder. Perhaps Tenskwatawa was better versed in the scientific literature of his day and knew of the impending eclipse when the governor did not. We will never know. But the outcome could not have done more to promote Tenskwatawa's mission. It turned the small village where it happened from a dot on the map of colonialism into a mecca for Native Americans.

Tenskwatawa announced that the Master of Life had instructed him to establish a New Jerusalem for his people. The words *New Jerusalem* are not his but mine. I call this vision of the Prophet a "Mecca" or a "New Jerusalem" or a "New Rome" to underscore what a radical notion it was for Native American culture. Native people have always had unique spiritual places or areas that they believe are sacred. Pyramid Lake in Nevada or the Black

Hills in South Dakota are good examples. But these were particular places for particular people; they were not universal holy sites that were to be revered by all nations. Tenskwatawa's new community, however, was intended to be exactly that kind of universal focus for a unified faith, embracing of all Native people and their traditions. It was like a Mecca, Jerusalem, or Rome: a city built on the hill for all to see, a rallying point for the faith, the seat of authority for all believers.

Symbolically, Tenskwatawa and Tecumseh chose the location of the prophet's village because it was ten miles over the border into American territory. When Governor Harrison carried out one of his land swindles, called the Treaty of Greenville, his surveyors had created a line between land still considered in Native possession and land reserved for white settlement. Since both of the Shawnee brothers rejected the Treaty of Greenville as fraudulent, they placed the holy town on land they considered sacred to the Shawnee and all other tribes. Located about two hundred miles southwest of modern Cleveland, Ohio, it would be a light on the hill, a beacon of resistance uniting all Native people.

A volunteer labor force went to work on construction of the new community in 1805. At the center was an immense, single-story whitewashed structure comprising hand-hewn posts, planks, rafters, and clapboard. When it was finished, it stood 150 feet long and 34 feet wide, facing the east. There were four large doors opening to the four directions on each side of the building. This was the great council house where worship and study of the new religion could be carried out.

Within a very short time, word of the holy village was spreading to Native nations up and down the Mississippi River. Soon long lines of pilgrims began moving toward Greenville. Government agents at American forts reported hundreds of Native people crossing the landscape on their way to the focal point of their faith. Anxiety increased as white people watched the town grow ever larger. Rumors about Greenville became wilder with the telling. The Prophet was gathering an army. A massive uprising was being planned. The Prophet was a madman. He was acting as an agent for the British in Canada. As one scholar has explained, these accusations by white colonizers "reflected their ignorance about the nature of his influence. Unable to comprehend the widespread frustration among the tribes, American officials refused to concede that Tenskwatawa's movement was an indigenous uprising, born of desperation. If they admitted that many of the Indian grievances were valid, they would be forced to address those most responsible: themselves. Of course they were unwilling to do so and therefore sought external causes for their domestic crisis."

Pressure on the American government to destroy the holy village increased in proportion to the number of Native converts coming to Greenville. By 1809 it seemed clear that armed conflict between the Shawnee brothers and Governor Harrison was inevitable. To face that conflict they would need as strong an alliance as they could build among the many Native nations, including those of the southern lands. Powerful nations like the Cherokee, Muskogee (Creek), Chickasaws, and Choctaws would need to be invited into a renewed vision similar to the one raised a generation before by Chief Pontiac and his prophet counterpart, Neolin.

Tecumseh was very clear that his ambition was to achieve what the United States itself had done: a unified nation created out of different constituencies. To do this he needed his brother's unifying spiritual vision and the visible sign of Native independence: the holy city on the hill. If war with Governor Harrison came too soon, if Greenville was destroyed, that might prove disastrous for the new pan-Native movement. It was too soon to fight, and Greenville was not the ditch to die in. The decision to move was made.

While Governor Harrison was preparing for an attack against Greenville, Tenskwatawa stepped sideways and disappeared, leaving the governor hanging in air with an army but no reason to fight. The Prophet did this by accepting the invitation of another great Native leader, Main Poc of the Potawatomi, to create a new holy village across the line outside American territory, on the Wabash, near its confluence with the Tippecanoe River. By doing so, he took all the wind out of Governor Harrison's warmongering.

Tenskwatawa personally oversaw the construction. A council house equal in proportions to the one in Greenville was erected, along with a new lodge called the House of the Stranger, designed as a welcome center for new converts. Within a very short time, the new community had grown even larger than Greenville, its beacon of Native American resistance glowing brighter for all to see. Tenskwatawa named his second New Jerusalem "Prophetstown," so there would be no mistaking where the seat of Native spiritual power resided.

Prophetstown, located just north of Lafayette, Indiana, became a lighthouse. As the Native nations in the borderlands between the Appalachians and the Mississippi were increasingly squeezed together by American land grabs, and as the apocalyptic pressures of epidemics and hunger increased, the communities faced the choice between assimilation, extinction, and diaspora. The American strategy of divide and conquer continued to isolate Native nations into ever smaller and weaker targets. Native people became refugees in their own land. In this context, the visible growth and unity of Prophetstown became a powerful apocalyptic symbol. It became the singularity of hope in the midst of a bleak landscape.

Thousands of Native people made the pilgrimage to listen to the prophet and return to their people with his message of reform and resistance. They abstained from alcohol, returned to the traditional values of communal life, and put aside old histories of conflict between Native cultures to embrace a new vision of Native American identity. Like St. Paul going out from Jerusalem to preach the new Christian religion, so Tecumseh went out from Prophetstown to preach Native solidarity. The Shawnee brothers had found the way to defeat American aggression: beat the Americans at their own game. If the Long Knives could weld their culture together into an unstoppable force, then the Native people could do the same to create an unmovable object.

Prophetstown was that object. As long as it existed, Native people had a center of spiritual gravity. In this community the apocalyptic revelation was made visible. People of many nations lived side by side in peace. They cooperated and worked together for the common good. They practiced their old traditions in a new way, revitalizing their sense of identity as God's people. They were a living model of what the future could be if only the people had faith. For the first time since the days of Pontiac and Neolin, it seemed the tide was turning. Americans were facing a war with Great Britain to the east, while to the west they were witnessing a transformation of Native America from a collection of tribes into a United States of Indigenous People. History was balanced on a symbol: as long as Prophetstown was free, Native people were free.

Which is why it had to be destroyed.

— • —

In 1811, Tecumseh was away recruiting support among the southern nations. Tirelessly, he had crisscrossed the length and breadth of the increasingly incendiary border between the Native nations and the United States. If he could succeed in the south among nations like the Choctaw, Cherokee, and Muskogee, as he had done in the north among the Delawares, Miamis, and Potawatomis, then he would connect the Native nations from the Gulf of Mexico to the Great Lakes. With material support from British allies in Canada and Spanish allies in Florida and Louisiana, he could finally draw a line in the sand that the Americans could not cross.

Tecumseh, however, was not the only one to connect those dots. While he was away on his southern travels, Governor Harrison determined that the time was right to attack Prophetstown and destroy it as a symbol of Native unity. Without Tecumseh's military leadership, the holy town would be vulnerable. Consequently, in November 1811, Harrison gathered an army of regular American troops and local white militia and crossed the line into Native territory. He marched his troops toward Prophetstown. Tenskwatawa recognized the danger his brother's absence implied for the community, and he tried to deflect Governor Harrison into a dialogue about the reasons for the unprovoked attack. But Harrison was not concerned with justifying his assault. He was in no mood to talk, but he did decide to encamp his army near Prophetstown rather than attacking directly on his arrival in the area. He pitched his tents near the Tippecanoe River.

That night, the warriors of Prophetstown from many different nations attacked the Americans' camp. Without Tecumseh to lead them, they had no coordinated command structure, only a martyr's tenacity of faith to drive off the invasion of their sacred community. A stiff battle ensued that claimed almost 20 percent of Harrison's forces. But in the light of the next day, it was clear that the Americans had held their ground and that the path to Prophetstown was open. Harrison's troops were too depleted to do much more than burn the town before limping home, but it did not matter. The damage was done. Prophetstown was reduced to ashes.

— • —

If this were a history book rather than a spiritual book, we would go on to detail the events that followed the burning of Prophetstown after the Battle of Tippecanoe. We would talk about how the brothers sought to regroup, how they sought a British alliance, how they fought during the War of 1812, and how, ultimately, their dream died. But this is not a history or biography of Tenskwatawa. This is an analysis of apocalypse—a case study for those of us who want to know how Native American spirituality rose from those ashes and survived. What is the revelation we can discover from this historic experience?

Many scholars point to the inability of Native American nations to cooperate, either because of their own innate cultural bias toward libertarianism or because of the effective American strategy of alcohol, greed, and intimidation. From my own vantage point, however, as a Native American I would look in a slightly different direction. I would look to the city on the hill.

One of the most enduring and universal apocalyptic visions is the sacred community. In the myths and visions of many religions there is the image of the ideal community, not only as it is projected into the future world of an afterlife but as it exists in the here and now. It is a symbol of heaven on earth. And it is proof that faith is real. So places like Jerusalem, Mecca, or even Shangri-La take on apocalyptic significance. They exist between reality and revelation. They embody a hope and an ideal, the kingdom of God on earth. Even if they are not yet perfect, they are still living evidence that the vision of such perfection is possible. The city on the hill keeps hope alive. It inspires us to believe in a better tomorrow, and it shows us the way to get there.

But where is our city on the hill today? Where do we look for reassurance that what we hope for is still possible? For many of us, places like Mecca or Jerusalem or Rome have become more political than prophetic. They are identified with a particular historic faith, not a vision that can unite all people. In fact, they seem more divisive than unifying. As for the Shangri-las we have invented for ourselves, the many utopian projects to create just the right commune or the perfect spiritual community, they have mostly withered away, like the Oneida Community, or collapsed into madness, like the Branch Davidians. Consequently, we are suspicious of the idea of community. Not only do we not see it shining as a beacon before us; we doubt it exists down here where we live our daily lives. In fact, we see community unraveling around us with an apocalyptic certainty. People no longer want to cooperate. We distrust one another. We need to look out for ourselves. The mindset of our age is turning away from community and toward survivalism.

It is ironic that the city on the hill most visible today may be the survivalist's bunker. Faced with an apocalyptic collapse of all the old institutions on which we once relied, the survivalist offers an ideal of a single escape pod. Today this option has become increasingly popular, especially for those who can afford to ride out an apocalypse in luxury fortresses. Self-sufficient, self-reliant, self-focused: the vision of weathering an apocalypse becomes a formula that abandons community for the best way to keep other people out.

The death of community is one of the great apocalyptic fears of our time. Most of us still know deep inside that we cannot survive without community, but we cannot seem to create it. Like the Native people living in the years before the War of 1812, we know that united we stand, divided we fall. But how do we become united? How do we learn again to care for one another, to work with one another, to trust one another?

The Shawnee brothers offer us a clue: build a Prophetstown. Confronted with an apocalyptic context that included a host of people with different languages, different traditions, and different expectations—many of whom had a history of mistrust and even conflict with one another—Tenskwatawa and Tecumseh had the vision to generate a working model of a spiritual alternative. In other words, they designed the prototype. Prophetstown was a visible lesson in faith. Every day it existed, it invited people from very different backgrounds to explore the possibility of a bigger reality.

Prophetstown was an adventure and an exploration. People literally walked for hundreds of miles just to see it, just to experience it. Today the site of Prophetstown is a park with a historical marker, but in its day, Prophetstown excited the imagination and inspired creativity among people far from its boundaries. It became a vision within itself, an apocalyptic hope that was shared by word of mouth as far west as the Pacific Ocean. The Shawnee brothers recognized a deep spiritual principle inherent in Native American tradition: to believe is to see.

Prophetstown was that principle put into action. The Prophet taught that if Native people would only believe in themselves again—believe they were the people chosen for this land, believe that they were related as a single community—then they would start to see the change for which they so desperately longed. They began in Greenville because Greenville was a place where Governor Harrison had defrauded their people. It was a tangible sign of American power. And yet, if people believed they could confront this power—if they believed fraudulent treaties could be overcome—then they would start to see their own power grow and justice grow with it. The first council house in Greenville was that belief made visible. Through it, the prophet announced a new beginning. His choice of location was intentional. It was a way to perform a healing exactly where the wound had been received. The

Treaty of Greenville had been a source of despair and shame. The Village of Greenville was a revelation of hope and pride.

When the holy village at Greenville was threatened, when Governor Harrison planned to burn it to the ground, Tenskwatawa demonstrated the resilience of his apocalyptic vision by showing his followers a very visible spiritual lesson: the city on the hill can be seen on any hill you choose. In other words, the vision was not glued to a particular geography. It was not a Mecca or Jerusalem that could not be moved without the faith around it collapsing; it was a vision based on a belief that any person could carry it with them wherever they went. He transferred the location without disturbing the belief. In Prophetstown the belief remained intact; in fact, it grew stronger. As long as the people believed in community, that community could go anywhere. Every village could become a city on the hill. Every Native person could be a citizen of this new vision. The lines on the map drawn so rigidly by the colonizers could be erased. Native sovereignty was not tied to space but to belief. It could exist anywhere at any time.

The revelation of the prophet was that wherever people are willing to believe together, they will begin to see the results of their faith start to take shape before them. No matter how great the forces threatening them, they can create an alternative. Each time they build a House of the

Stranger to welcome others, they make their hope come to life.

While Tenskwatawa and Tecumseh did not live to see their vision completed with a United States of Indigenous People, they were able to release that vision into the hearts of their people for generations to come. All across North America, wherever people talked about the Prophet and about his sacred village, the belief in Native sovereignty and unity began to grow. The transportable vision that was so rooted in Greenville and Prophetstown was implanted in the consciousness of thousands of Native people—so much so that even when the actual village was destroyed by the oppressor, it survived in the minds of the believers. And because they believed, they saw. They saw themselves in a new way—not as isolated tribes, but as a people. One people. One great Indigenous people living by the faith their ancestors had given them. That belief never left them, even when they were forced to move.

— • —

And they were forced to move. The years following the War of 1812 are characterized as the time of "Removal" for the Native nations east of the Mississippi. One by one, following the original plan of Thomas Jefferson, the remaining nations were forced off their land and sent to the West. The Shawnee went to live on a narrow strip of Kansas. Tenskwatawa went with them. His brother had died during the war, fighting alongside the British in Canada, at the Battle of the Thames in 1813. He died a hero's death, standing his ground against overwhelming odds, facing his enemy. He was buried in an unknown grave, a legend in his own time as well as ours.

Tenskwatawa survived but was a sad figure to those who saw him. He still had many followers, but the network of their community was fractured by the loss of the war. Tenskwatawa was exiled from the United States. He was marginalized and cut off from his family and his supporters. By 1825, he was considered harmless enough to be allowed back into the United States from his exile in Canada. In 1828 he joined his people on their removal to the Kansas reservation.

In the autumn of 1832, a young painter named George Catlin asked if he could paint the prophet's portrait to preserve it for history, and Tenskwatawa agreed because that is all he thought he had become: a footnote in history. The painting shows him dressed in his clothes as the prophet, a turban and feathers, long earrings and bracelets, holding his "medicine fire," a carved stick with feathers and wampum beads. Catlin's portrait, like that of so many Native leaders he painted, captures the end of an era in America, the last glimpse of men and women who lived through the American Apocalypse.

But for me, as a Native person, Catlin's painting does not have the last word on the prophet. That word is reserved for what Tenskwatawa called the four small cabins where he lived out the rest of his life in obscurity with his family. What did he name the little spot where he lived out his last days? Prophetstown.

Even after the destruction of the two predecessor villages, even after the loss of the war against the Americans, and even after the death of his brother, Tenskwatawa was defiant to the end. He carried his belief in his heart, so what he saw was that belief coming alive wherever he went. Therefore, Prophetstown was wherever Tenskwatawa was. The city on the hill was within him.

I believe the same can be true of us. Living now in an apocalyptic process of our own, we can each choose to carry the light of a Prophetstown within us. We can embody the city on the hill that shows us a better alternative is possible. We can be brought together into community, even though we think of ourselves as strangers. We can find our place in the House of the Stranger, a meeting place for us to learn from one another and grow together in a shared faith. We can begin to see change because we believe in change.

I know this is true because, in a very small way, I was able to live into Tenskwatawa's vision. I did it in the unlikeliest of places and in a way Tenskwatawa could never have imagined. But I believe my experience illustrates a new way to see an old vision.

In 2011 I began writing small daily messages on a giant social media platform that has millions of subscribers. My messages were spiritual in nature, but open to people of any faith tradition, or even of no particular faith at all. When I began writing these little meditations, only a few sentences each, I had a readership of four people. As I write these words today, there are tens of thousands of people in my community, and it is still growing, all from a wide variety of cultures.

Because I am an elder, I cannot predict if my online page will still be going as you read these words, but that is not the important point of my sharing. How long I last on social media or how many people ultimately notice my writing is only bean counting. The real spiritual point is that my experience shows how Tenskwatawa's vision works as well today as it did in 1807. I have the prototype to prove it.

My location was not beside a river in Ohio but beside a global information river online. My message was like the Prophet's teachings: a call for peace, love, and justice. Like the Prophet, my goal was to unite people of many backgrounds. Like Tenskwatawa, I welcomed people to follow the traditions of their ancestors but to do so in community with others from all walks of life. I set up my meeting house on the high hill of the internet, where everyone could see it, and I invited others to join me in a new community where we could live in peace and with integrity.

And it worked. Not because I am a prophet but because I followed the Prophet's lead. I created a tangible place, even in the heart of the beast, where people from any tribe could hear words of renewal and hope. I left the doors of the meeting house wide open to all Four Sacred Directions. I offered a prototype. I offered an alternative. I encouraged people to share the message in their own Prophetstown, words of welcome and solidarity that could unite us all, not only up and down the Mississippi but all around the world.

I am no Tenskwatawa, and my books have not saved humanity from an apocalypse, but I believe they have helped. I believe, in a modest way, I have done what I can to be a city on the hill that others can see and, in seeing, take heart and believe in our combined future. I have not single-handedly brought renewal and restoration to the world, but I have been one more tiny proof that renewal is possible. My Prophetstown is still standing, still visible, and even after I am history, it will go on, because I have planted it in other hearts on other hills I cannot even see.

We will not overcome any apocalypse alone but only in community. I think we all subconsciously understand that. What has caused us to stumble is the fear that we have forgotten how to live together in mutual respect and unity. That is why the unique decision of Tenskwatawa to create a tangible focus for his people is so important. It gives us the awareness that we can do the same thing. We can plant communities of hope all around the world. We can do it through the use of a technology that the two Shawnee brothers would have been delighted to use if it had existed in their apocalyptic time. All of us, wherever we live, can begin building our own version of Prophetstown: communities open to all without exception, communities based on diversity and respect, communities believing enough together to begin seeing together.

4

SMOHALLA

If the Land Has Anything to Say

As though scanning a battlefield, Howard assayed the individual before him: "a large headed, hump-shouldered, odd little wizard of an Indian . . . a strange mixture of timidity and daring, of superstition and intelligence. Howard observed of Smohalla that he was "short and shapeless . . . scarcely any neck; bandy legs, rather long for his body."
. . . He further noted that although Smohalla was deformed and was the strangest human being that he had ever seen, the Dreamer had a finely formed head, expressive, magnetic eyes that contrasted with his head covering, two corners of which were tied under his chin.

—Robert H. Ruby and John A. Brown

ONE OF THE most poignant stories of the American Apocalypse is that of Chief Joseph of the Nez Perce. His people were part of the Shapatian language group, which included other Native nations around the Columbia Plateau within the modern-day states of Washington, Oregon, and Idaho. Nations such as the Cayuses, Palouses, Sinkiuses, and Yakima were communities intimately connected to the rivers that were a major source of food in this otherwise arid landscape. They were salmon fishers as well as deer hunters, and the abundance of fish and game provided them with a large and stable economy.

This was land that Lewis and Clark crossed on their way to the Pacific in 1805. It was a major focus for the Hudson Bay Company, which sent trappers and traders into the region in the 1820s and 1830s from Fort Vancouver on the Columbia River. By the 1850s, so many settlers and miners had followed this well-worn trail of western expansion into the Columbia Plateau that the once fertile homeland of the Indigenous people was becoming something else entirely. Land speculators, railroad magnates, and commercial fishing companies had carved it up into slices for their own interests.

The American government demanded that all Indigenous nations be forced onto small reservations, and inevitably the people fought back. The Yakima War of 1855–1858 was a long and bloody conflict throughout Washington territory and beyond. The impact of that conflict was still being felt in 1877 when General Oliver Howard gave the

Nez Perce an ultimatum: either move onto the reservation or consider yourself at war with the United States.

Chief Joseph rejected that ultimatum, for religious reasons. He was a follower of the Dreamer religion, a spiritual tradition based on shamanistic visions. He held the earth as sacred—too sacred to be sold for a few pieces of silver or gold. The land on which the Nez Perce lived was the resting place of his ancestors and was holy ground that could not be bartered away. As he tried to explain to the Americans who had come to demand his submission,

> My father sent for me. I saw he was dying. I took his hand in mine. He said: My son, my body is returning to my mother earth, and my spirit is going very soon to see the Great Spirit Chief. When I am gone, think of your country. You are the chief of these people. They look to you to guide them. Always remember that your father never sold his country. You must stop your ears whenever you are asked to sign a treaty to sell your home. A few years more, and white men will be all around you. They have their eyes on this land. My son, never forget my dying words. This country holds your father's body. Never sell the bones of your father and mother. I pressed my father's hand and told him I would protect his grave with my life. My father smiled and passed away to the spirit-land.

Rather than break his vow, Chief Joseph led his people on a desperate escape. The whole nation attempted to reach the Canadian border. There they hoped to find religious freedom. They wanted to join Sitting Bull, who had brought many of the Lakota to safety, preferring to live as refugees than be guilty of giving away their birthright. For weeks the Nez Perce moved north, fighting a rearguard action over and over again as General Howard and his troops relentlessly pursued them. Many of the elders and children died on the journey. Finally, only forty miles from the border, Chief Joseph and his starving people were cornered in Montana. His words to the general are considered one of the deepest expressions of Native American thought ever recorded:

Tell General Howard I know his heart. What he told me before I have in my heart. I am tired of fighting. Our chiefs are killed. Looking Glass is dead. Too-hul-hul-sote is dead. The old men are all dead. It is the young men who say yes or no. He who led the young men is dead. It is cold and we have no blankets. The little children are freezing to death. My people, some of them, have run away to the hills, and have no blankets, no food; no one knows where they are—perhaps freezing to death. I want to have time to look for my children and see how many of them I can find. Maybe I shall find them among the dead. Hear me my chiefs. I am tired; my heart is sick and sad. From where the sun now stands I will fight no more forever.

What was it that could inspire not just one man but a whole nation to undertake such a noble but tragic flight to freedom? What gave them the courage and dignity to defy overwhelming odds and remain true to their principles even in the midst of an apocalypse? The answer may seem strange, but it is accurate: they were following a dream.

That dream was contained in the *Washani*, a word that translates from the Shapitian word for "dancers." The Washani creed had grown up among all the peoples of the Columbia Plateau over the many years from Lewis and Clark to Chief Joseph. In many respects, the Washani creed was almost identical to the traditions of other Native American nations, including those whose prophets are the subject of this book. Like the Seneca, the Shawnee, and the Paiute, these people knew a long history of visionary travels by spiritual leaders. Entering a trance, being visited by heavenly messengers, and making the astral journey to the afterlife was common to all these cultures. The distance between earth and heaven was crossed by bridges, such as the Milky Way. It was not unusual for someone to claim they had made the trip, because the concept of the vision quest was so strong in Native tradition.

While the Americans came from a culture where receiving visions from heaven was reserved for only a select few and most of those historical figures from the distant past, among Native American communities, seeking a personal vision from a higher power was a common expectation. Men and women regularly made a retreat into the natural world to seek divine guidance. After a period of preparation, such as prayer and purification, they would go to an isolated place to fast and wait for a vision. These visions were taken very seriously, because they were thought to show people their true path in life. The Washani creed, therefore, was a widespread part of Native American religion.

It was expressed by the Washat dance, the physical sign of the deeper spiritual bond that existed between Nami Piap, the Creator, the Earth Mother, and the many nations of human beings on the Columbia Plateau. The Washani creed was the traditional faith among the *yantcha*: the men and women who had "died" in a trance, gone to heaven, and returned with messages for the community. These were the Dreamers, and their faith was expressed in the Washat dances and songs they brought to their people.

Among these many Dreamers was one in particular who stands out: Smohalla, a yantcha from the small Wanapams community that occupied land at a place called Priest Rapids on the Columbia River. Around the year 1850, Smohalla began to experience the dream state that took him to a higher dimension of reality. As a young man he had made his own vision quest to the sacred mountain La Lac, where he received his *wot*, his guardian spirit. But his journeys to heaven became even more intense. He made the mystic journey to heaven and was informed that an apocalypse was coming, a revelation that would herald a great change for all Indigenous people. Therefore, it was critical that Native people from every nation in North America return to their ancestral ways and abandon any reliance on the ways of the white people.

Smohalla's guidance was clear: Native people were to give up the technology and clothing of the colonizers. They were to go back to hunting and fishing as they had once done before the introduction of firearms. Like all of the four prophets, Smohalla stressed this need to divest from white culture in an intentional way. But in one aspect of this return to the old traditions, Smohalla was adamant. He came to understand that "a holy covenant existed between God and man, and that to maintain this relationship, the Indians must not disturb the earth by dividing it into parcels, by farming, or by selling any portion of land."

The prohibition against farming may seem odd to our contemporary sensibilities, which equate farming with a peaceful and life-sustaining vocation. But for Native American prophets, farming was sacrilegious. It was contrary to the covenant the Creator had made with the Native people when Nami Piap first chose them to live on their land. In Native spirituality, the cultivation of the land was one of the sacred activities of women. The corn they planted or the roots and berries they harvested were part of the natural cycle of life. As life-givers, women planted the seeds and gathered the produce as an expression of their relationship with Mother Earth. Men, on the other hand, were hunters who harvested fish and game. This role balanced that of the women and required that men remain spiritually in kinship with the creatures they sought for food. Farming, especially in the way and on the scale suggested by the white people, overturned and violated this ancient equilibrium. It displaced women from their historic position, forced men to lose their identity as hunters, and scrambled the kinship ties between human beings and the rest of creation.

By 1850, the American solution to the "Indian problem" was described as the Plow and Bible approach. The strategy was simple: turn Native Americans into serf farmers on 160-acre plots of land on militarized reservations they could not leave; open up the rest to white settlement; take their children away for re-education at boarding schools; and christianize the Native people to erase their culture and assimilate them into the dominant way of life. In effect, it was a strategy of gradual apocalypse: a slow, downward spiral into cultural oblivion. As one historian has described it, "Nothing resulting from the American presence caused the tribes more anguish than did confinement on reservations for the 'crime' of standing in the way of advancing Americans. Under governmental protection, whites appropriated and exploited Indian lands, some of which were sacred, and ancient subsistence patterns were destroyed in the process. Fenced off tracts interfered with passage to traditional grazing, root, berry, and fishing grounds."

The apocalypse unfolding on the Columbia Plateau not only involved cultural extinction but epidemic diseases like smallpox and measles, physical attacks and murders by white settlers, and military campaigns throughout what came to be called the Yakima War from 1855 to 1858. It was into this cauldron of apocalyptic crisis that Dreamer prophets like Smohalla sought to offer Native people an alternative of hope.

Like so many other Native American spiritual leaders, Smohalla drew on the ancient traditions of his people as the foundation for his new faith. The covenant triangle between the Creator, the earth, and human beings was the core of his teachings. He taught that the traditions of maintaining balance between the three must be maintained. But given the depth of the crisis faced by the people of the Plateau, more was needed. New expressions of the old faith must be released if genocide was to be avoided.

— • —

In his visionary journeys to the spirit world, Smohalla received an expanded understanding of the traditional Washani creed. He returned from his dream state with new dances and songs to express the path to salvation. In his village by the Priest Rapids he erected a Longhouse where these ceremonies, the Washat ceremonies, could be performed. He raised a flag of his own design representing the four sacred directions inherent in all Native American religious beliefs: the yellow grass, green mountains, blue sky, and red heart.

He instructed the people in new dances. The men and women would dance opposite one another to represent the balance between them, and as they danced they would hold small bells, which would be the sound of their coming redemption. For when Nami Piap returned at the impending apocalypse to drive away the Americans and restore the Native nations, it would be to the sound of a great bell. The seven drums, the "pom-pom" drums, were used in the dances to sound the heartbeat of creation in which the people could take shelter.

In these new Washat celebrations, the people would physically embody the vision of their future. They would actively resist the evil surrounding them and push back the tide of American destruction. As they danced, they chanted the new songs Smohalla brought them, simple Zen-like lyrics and yet with a deep meaning for Washani theology:

Sound of the bell
Sound of the heart
My brothers
My sisters
I am meeting you
I am meeting you at the dance.

Like other Native American prophets, Smohalla was
labeled a fraud by the American authorities and press.
They blamed Smohalla and his new Washat dances for stirring up discontent. They claimed he was the mastermind
behind all Native acts of resistance. On several occasions
they sought to force him to agree to treaties, but each
time Smohalla outmaneuvered the Americans and kept
his small community off the reservation. He would meet
with the American negotiators on reservation lands, out-
debate them and shame them, camp there until they were
gone, and then return to the Columbia, where his people,
the Wanapams, the River People, would continue to live as
they had for centuries.

In every regard, Smohalla rejected settler culture. He
did not want their money, their annuities, their schools,
their technology, or their churches. He was an icono-
clast. He did not see any value in what they offered him.
Instead, he preached the old values of his ancestors.
While other yantcha upheld the same message, Smohalla

became the most widely revered. His integrity and tenacity, as well as his reputation for outsmarting the aggressors, won him converts throughout the Plateau and as far away as Nevada and the Dakotas. The Washat dances spread far and wide, creating more anxiety among the American authorities.

The irony of the Dreamer religion is that it was perceived in such diametrically different ways by those who encountered it. White people saw it as a dangerous and pernicious cult that incited Native people to acts of violence. For the Indigenous people, it was a faith of peaceful expectation, a message of care and protection for the third member of the ancient covenant triangle: Mother Earth. In one exchange with a government agent, Smohalla expressed the dichotomy between his people's way of seeing things and that of the American settlers:

> We simply take the gifts that are freely offered. We no more harm the earth than would an infant's fingers harm its mother's breast. But the white man tears up large tracts of land, runs deep ditches, cuts down forests, and changes the whole face of the earth. You know very well this is not right. Every honest man knows in his heart that this is all wrong. But the white men are so greedy they do not consider these things.

Smohalla never advocated violence. He never engaged in war, even if he felt the pain that caused his people to resist. He continued to believe in a higher level of justice. He trusted Nami Piap to restore the balance of life among his people in supernatural ways. Like the pom-pom drums, his message was the heartbeat of the Columbia Plateau. People believed there was still hope as long as Smohalla could hold out against white domination.

The influence of Smohalla explains the nonviolent actions of followers like Chief Joseph, who sought to buy time for divine intervention rather than make a suicidal charge against the guns of the American military. The poignancy of Chief Joseph's desperate escape plan underscores the peaceful nature of the Dreamer faith and its concern to treat the land as sacred. Essentially the two cultural views, settler and Native, were incompatible. White people saw nature as resources to be extracted and used. Native people saw nature as a personal relationship, a trust to be maintained. Smohalla was clear in his rejection of the American view:

You asked me to plough the ground! Shall I take a knife and tear my mother's bosom? Then when I die she will not take me to her bosom to rest. You ask me to dig for stone! Shall I dig under her skin for her bones? Then when I die I cannot enter her body to be born again. You ask me to cut the grass, make hay and sell it, and be rich like white men, but how dare I cut off my mother's hair?

Reading the language Smohalla used in his ceaseless arguments with the American authorities of his time is a bit like watching a melodrama. His language is dramatic, emotional, almost over the top for our contemporary culture. He can sound like a quaint reminder of a lost vision, interred now with the bones of Chief Joseph's father and mother.

But however heartfelt his words may have been, it is the silent image of Smoholla himself, standing alone, unmovable in his faith, that captures attention. His dignified silence is worth listening to. From 1850 until his death in 1895, Smohalla never capitulated to American demands. He never recanted his religious beliefs, never lived on a reservation. He remained true to his traditions long after others had given up and given in. When the other communities around him had been broken, moved to reservations, and forced to give their children to the boarding schools, Smohalla remained quietly independent. He kept his flag of the Washani creed flying. He stayed in the backwater of Priest Rapids living as he always lived, reminding others that they could live this way too.

History passed him by, and he became more of a curiosity than a threat to the dominant culture. He became an anachronism, but he was still standing. He was still an alternative to business as usual in the American economic system. He offered people a choice, even if only a handful of them would choose to take it.

— • —

Smohalla's choice is still here. To engage it, all we have to do is look at what we have most in common with his vision. It is not a quantum leap. What Smohalla had to say about the earth is as current as the latest scientific reports on the death of our planet. Smohalla's call to recognize the earth as a living being resonates with our contemporary ecological crises. The Washani creed is still here for any of us who want to join the prophet in fending off an environmental apocalypse. It is the choice to reconsider the fundamental relationship we have to the earth.

As I am writing these words, the United Nations' Intergovernmental Panel on Climate Change (IPCC) has just released another apocalyptic report:

The world's leading climate scientists on Monday warned human-induced climate change is causing dangerous and widespread disruption in nature, with people and ecosystems least able to cope being the hardest hit. The highly anticipated report from the U.N.'s IPCC, approved by 195 member states, makes clear that minor, reactive or incremental changes are no longer sufficient to tackle the climate emergency. The analysis provides world leaders with a gold standard summation of modern climate science. . . . It says the world faces unavoidable climate hazards in the next two decades with global heating of 1.5 degrees Celsius above pre-industrial levels. . . . Even temporarily exceeding this critical threshold, the report says, would result in additional severe impact.

One of the surreal things about the environmental apocalypse is that we see it coming. In fact, it is already here. The polar ice is melting. Water levels are rising. Weather patterns are changing. Droughts and storms are intensifying. Crops are failing. Yet even as reports like this one keep coming out, sounding the alarm over and over like the ringing of a bell, our response is slow, almost sporadic, as affluent nations seek to meet the crisis while maintaining their standard of living. In the meantime, poorer nations continue to destroy their own ecology in an attempt to reach those inflated standards. A truly united, consistent, and sustainable response eludes us. We seem stuck in the headlights of an oncoming disaster without knowing how to move.

Perhaps the Dreamer can show us an answer. Not in more scientific reports but in a spiritual shift of the heart. In the covenant at the core of the Washani creed, Smohalla employed very graphic language to describe Mother

Earth. He equated the relationship between the earth and human beings with the reality of any mother who has given birth and raised children. He describes activities such as mining or farming as a violation of her body. In this way Smohalla, like many other Native American prophets, sought to anthropomorphize the earth as a living being with whom we have a very intimate relationship. He used dramatic language to create this imagery precisely because his opponents, the American business and military interests, used just the reverse: they sought to negotiate on the basis of inanimate objects, natural resources, and financial quantifiability. There was no room in their worldview for a personal relationship with the land or the rivers. They were just things. Things to be plowed up, cut down, or dug out. The utilitarian vision of the environment was as far as they could, or were willing, to see.

Smohalla's vision was very different. One of his followers, Young Chief of the Cayuses, expressed that alternative vision in 1855 during a debate over land with Isaac Stevens, the territorial governor of Washington: "I wonder," Young Chief said, "if this land has anything to say? I wonder if the ground is listening to what is said? I wonder if the ground would come to life and what is on it; though I hear what the Earth says: the Earth says, God has placed me here."

Young Chief is pointing to the missing voice in the land negotiation. He is asking if the earth herself has anything to say in the conversation. He is inviting the governor to notice that a key player has not been invited to the table. The covenant triangle between the Creator, the earth, and humans is broken because Mother Earth is not being heard.

For adherents of the Dreamer religion, these are not romantic or poetic images but genuine spiritual concerns. The Washani creed is the belief in a single Creator who created a single life. That single life is the earth. The earth is a single living being in relationship with her maker. As human beings, we are only a small part of the total life of the earth, but we are special—chosen, you might say—because we have the self-awareness to be one step removed from the earth. We can step to one side spiritually or intellectually, and observe the other two parts of the triangle. We can relate to the Creator. We can relate to the earth. And the nature of those relationships is what we can describe as the Washani covenant.

In the ancient traditions of Judaism, the idea of humanity existing in a special relationship to God is foundational. The people of Israel are a chosen people, destined to occupy a sacred land, which they hold in trust in a covenant (agreement) with God. Exactly the same vision developed in Native America over the millennia of our life in North America. Like ancient Israel, ancient Native American theology understood a covenant relationship between God, the earth, and humanity. The two religious concepts are almost identical. Native American nations believed they were the people chosen to live in a promised land. They understood that they occupied this land in a spiritual agreement with the Creator. They were stewards of the land, not true owners. Their existence on the land was a matter of sacred relationship, the mutual recognition of a covenant grounded in faith and worship.

The two religious worldviews part company, however, with regard to the third member of the covenant triangle: the role and nature of the earth. Native American spirituality has a more nuanced and sophisticated vision of the earth as a living ecosystem. Land is not just dirt and rocks but the outer skin of a living being. The earth is alive. It breathes. It grows. It dies. It is a being of infinite parts, just as humans are, and like humans, it has a spirit.

Perhaps their strictly monotheistic tradition kept ancient Israel from seeing the land, the earth, as a being worthy of voice and consideration. But Native American spiritual systems did not share that anxiety. The Washani creed is monotheistic, just like most every Indigenous religious community in North America, but it includes a carefully calibrated understanding of the relationship the Creator has with the creation. That relationship is not just between Creator and humanity, in which all the other partners are silent, but between Creator, humanity, and the earth. All the stakeholders must be at the table in the process we call life.

From the Native American viewpoint, without that third member of the covenant, the religion becomes a two-legged stool. Something critical, as Young Chief tried to point out, is missing. The third leg of the covenant is the relationship to every aspect of life embodied in the spiritual metaphor of Mother Earth. Human beings may be self-aware, they may even be the people chosen to occupy a particular niche in creation, but they are only a small part of the whole story, and not always even the most important characters of that story.

This acceptance of the earth as a conscious partner in the covenant of life helps us as human beings to avoid the arrogance and greed that Smohalla believed was the blindness of the white people who laughed at his vision of the earth as a living woman. Part of our inability to move out of the way of an environmental apocalypse is hubris, an overwhelming sense of pride in our own self-worth. From the traditional Native perspective, contemporary American culture lacks any sense of humility. Having been raised in the privileged fantasy that we are immune to consequences and able to invent solutions to every crisis, we lack the ability to trust in the Creator or to honor the Mother. We reduce our situation to a one-legged stool. We depend only on ourselves. We violate our ancient covenant and, eventually according to Smohalla, we will pay for our pride. In fact, we are already paying.

"Men who work," Smohalla once said, "cannot dream, and wisdom comes to us in dreams." He was talking about people who cannot see beyond their own utilitarian desires—people who cannot see the forest for the trees. They concentrate on what they need for the moment. They think of what will bring them more comfort and more leisure. They are constantly busy building wealth and power. These are people who have been raised in a culture of more. Always wanting more, needing more, taking more, and usually only for themselves. The old values of the Washani—values like sharing and equality—are lost in the stampede for more. Consequently, these people have no wisdom. They can see the apocalypse coming, but they cannot imagine how to prevent it. Their equivocation is their destiny.

— • —

Many years ago, in 2007, I had a vision to change that destiny. I had a dream. Ironically, I first shared it in Seattle, Washington, not far from where Smohalla lived and taught. On February 24 of the following year I stood in the pulpit of the National Cathedral in Washington, DC, to announce my dream to the world and invite others to see it too.

Without realizing it, I was following in the path of the prophet. Like Smohalla, I believed that our Mother Earth was under threat. And like Smohalla, I embraced the ancient covenant of our people as a way to save her, to save all of us, from the apocalypse of environmental collapse. In my sermon I spoke about that collapse as scientists around the world were already seeing it coming. I spoke about climate change and global warming, about rising sea levels and a toxic air. Then, without realizing it, I instinctively used Smohalla's Dreamer language:

Who will save us? Who will act? When the need is so great. The time is short. Who will do this for us? Whom shall we send? Whom shall we look to for our salvation?

I had a vision. Listen. I had a dream. Listen.

There is an answer. There is the beginning of an answer. Where will it come from? From communities of faith. From people who believe in something greater than themselves. From spiritual people. From religious people. From those of us who care enough to stand up and to act together to effect change and to make things different because we are people of faith. Because we believe in something and have the courage and the resolve to act and live through that faith.

I had a vision. I had a dream. I saw in my mind's eye a simple question begin to dawn. And I believe it was from God.

I went on to describe the vision I had dreamed to create a covenant between every religious community in the United States. My dream was to see all faith communities make a single witness together: to cut the greenhouse gas emissions from every property they owned by 50 percent in ten years or less. Every church, every synagogue, every mosque, every temple. Every school, every hospital, every office building owned and operated by religious communities. Jews, Christians, Buddhists, Hindus, Muslims: a united front to save the planet. In my dream the spiritual leaders of all these faith communities would appear together in the global media, standing side by side, saying that while we, people of faith, may disagree about many things, on this one issue we are absolutely united. We all acknowledge the danger, and we all take part in the solution. We set aside our differences for the common good.

What impact would that have? I asked that question in my sermon and offered an answer: it would be an apocalyptic revelation that the media could not ignore. The message of unity and harmony among people of different religions would make headlines around the world. It would inspire similar actions in other countries. It would invite internationally recognized spiritual leaders to step up to the microphone to offer support for this worldwide effort of faith.

In time, such a visible momentum in the struggle to combat climate change would draw in other sectors of the global society. Corporations, for example, would feel the need to be seen doing their part too. Political parties would be expected to offer their endorsement. Universities and medical facilities would be drawn into the expanding vision of a shared response. In my dream I saw how faith communities could become the catalyst for a truly effective reply to the threat of an ecological apocalypse. We would be the spark to light the fire of change. And all we had to do was cooperate. Acknowledge our relationship to Mother Earth. Accept our role in maintaining that relationship. Stand up together and be counted.

I called my dream the Genesis Covenant. I shared it publicly in as many places as I could, and I invited others from every faith community to join me in lobbying their community to embrace the vision. In 2009 my own denomination, the Episcopal Church, passed a Genesis Covenant resolution at our national convention. We went on record. We took the pledge to lower our greenhouse gas emissions and carbon footprint. I believed many other religious communities would soon join us and my dream of a united front would begin to unfold like a revelation.

— • —

It never happened. While many said they were concerned about environmental issues and working on it in their own way, there was no unified response to the level I had dreamed: a stage filled with religious leaders of every description, all calling for a global response to this shared danger. The momentum I hoped to begin never got rolling. My dream of seeing Roman Catholic bishops standing next to Southern Baptist preachers, beside Jewish rabbis and Buddhist monks, with imams and Hindu gurus never materialized. What I thought would be such a simple and obvious solution—getting religious people to share in doing the right thing for the sake of the humanity they served—was left hanging in air. Like a mist, it soon evaporated as everyone got back to doing their own thing separately.

Did the failure of my Genesis Covenant miss an opportunity to change our destiny? I think so. I still believe, as Smohalla always believed, that acknowledging our intimate relationship to the earth is the beginning of wisdom. The dream I had would have produced more than environmental action: it would have demonstrated a foundation for peace beyond anything we had seen to date, or that we have seen since all these years later. That stage full of diverse religious leaders would have sent a message of peace and nonviolence around the world. It would have visibly demonstrated that while we can argue about theology, when it comes to caring for our planet and our people, we are always together.

Not all dreams work in daylight. Smohalla was left standing on his historic stage alone. His dreams for the restoration of Native American traditional life were lost in other agendas, agendas of conflict and control. But that doesn't mean he failed. Smohalla was, like Ganiodaiio, Tenskwatawa, and as we shall see, Wovoka, a shooting star of the apocalyptic process. He rose from obscurity, burned brightly at a time of enormous crisis, and then slowly descended back into obscurity. Whether they were like shooting stars or not, these prophets shared a very similar trajectory. They made the same journey over the Milky Way. They visited heaven, received a mission, and returned to carry it out. And because their words were so powerful for the people of their time, they were both remembered and revered. They left their handprint in the mind and soul of Native America.

I hope I have done the same. My own dream may not have made it to the light of day, but that does not mean the effort was a failure. It is not too late. It is never too late to do what is right and holy.

The Genesis Covenant was the projection of the traditional Native American dream into the harsh realities of our own time. It may not have worked then, any more than Smohalla was able to do in his time, but there is no reason it cannot work now. That is the power of faith. We need to follow the example of the prophet and keep his flag flying. My dream may have faded, but it is still there. The dreamer may die, but the Dream does not.

Mother Earth is a living being. She has a heart. She has a spirit. When we recognize her for who she is, we open the door of our souls to welcome her as our Mother. And once enough of us have made that intimate connection with her, once we have accepted our covenant with life, the quicker we will act with a common intention. Like siblings of one great Mother, we will stand up for what is right. We will make the changes and the sacrifices that will be needed if our Mother is to be healed. Therefore, our task is clear. We are to strive diligently with every means at our disposal to awaken people to one fundamental spiritual truth: if we do not believe the earth is alive, we do not believe she must be saved.

The key to stopping the environmental apocalypse is not science but love. For decades now we have been staring at the scientific reports. They have not sufficiently inspired us to change our apocalyptic reality. But where science has failed, faith can succeed. We must help humanity rediscover their loving parent, the living world that sustains them. We must help them feel her love just as we show them how that love can be returned. And it can begin by gathering people around two simple questions: Where were you in nature when you experienced a vision of such beauty that it took your breath away? And how did that make you feel? If you can answer those two questions, you are on your way to meeting the Mother you may never have known before.

I wonder if the ground is aware of what I am writing?

I wonder if the earth has anything to say?

5

WOVOKA

To Go beyond What We Think Is Possible

As he approached I saw that he was a young man, a dark full blood, compactly built, and taller than the Paiute generally, being nearly 6 feet in height. He was well dressed in white man's clothes, with the broad-brimmed white felt hat common in the west, secured on his head by means of a beaded ribbon under the chin. He wore a good pair of boots. His hair was cut off square on a line below the base of the ears, after the manner of his tribe. His countenance was open and expressive of firmness and decision . . . the features were broad and heavy, very different from the thin, clear-cut features of the prairie tribes.

—James Mooney

MORE THAN EIGHTY years after it ended, the Ghost Dance came to haunt me in a vision. The memory of it whispered to me to join the dance. The year was 1973. At a place called Wounded Knee a small group of Native American activists were in a stand-off with the federal government. They were members of the American Indian Movement, AIM, and they had occupied the community of Wounded Knee in South Dakota to protest the ongoing oppression of the Lakota people on the Pine Ridge Reservation and all Indigenous peoples throughout Indian Country.

Like most every Native person at that time I was galvanized to the drama of the siege as federal marshals, FBI agents, and state police surrounded the protestors. It was a staple on the evening news and made international headlines. It educated a new generation to the dark history of the American Apocalypse and inspired Native activists like me to stand up and be counted for our ancestors.

For seventy-one days the AIM warriors held out, with people on both sides being killed. But by April when a young Lakota man, Lawrence "Buddy" Lamont, who was well loved in the local community, was killed by a government sniper and buried in a traditional way by his comrades, the elders called for an end to the conflict. The siege was lifted. The participants went home.

But the historic message of this moment was not lost. The AIM leadership, Russell Means and Dennis Banks, had chosen Wounded Knee for a reason: it was already a landmark on the map of Native American resistance to white domination. In 1890 it had been the scene of one of the most tragic events in American history. Some two hundred Native people were massacred by the 7th Cavalry Regiment, many machine-gunned down by the Hotchkiss guns that were the rapid-fire artillery of their time.

One of the earliest descriptions of this genocide comes from an ethnologist from the Smithsonian Institution, James Mooney, who recorded the aftermath in stark details:

> On New Year's day of 1891, three days after the battle, a detachment of troops was sent out to Wounded Knee to gather up and bury the Indian dead. . . . The bodies of the slaughtered men, women and children were found lying about under the snow, frozen stiff and covered in blood. Almost all the dead warriors were lying about Big Foot's tipi, but the women and children were found scattered along for 2 miles from the scene of the encounter, showing they had been killed while trying to escape. Four babies were found alive under the snow, wrapped in shawls and lying beside their dead mothers, whose last thought had been of them. They were all badly frozen and only one lived.

The dead were buried in a mass grave. None of the local Christian clergy came out to offer any prayers. Many of the soldiers responsible for the slaughter were awarded the

Congressional Medal of Honor to symbolize the final "victory" of the 7th Cavalry over the Native nations who had so decisively defeated them at Little Big Horn under George Armstrong Custer in 1876. The difference, of course, is that in 1876 the Native people could defend themselves, where in 1890 at Wounded Knee most were defenseless. The victory the 7th Calvalry won was over women trying to protect their babies.

There are many in-depth studies of the great tragedy at Wounded Knee, but since our goal is not to write another history but rather to search for deeper meanings, we can bring the focus down to a single question: What were these people doing to have deserved such a heartrending fate? What was their offense?

The answer: they were guilty of dancing.

The Lakota people who were machine-gunned down in the snow were believers in a new religion that had been sweeping through Native nations at the end of the nineteenth century. They were followers of the prophet Wovoka, and they were worshiping in the way he had instructed them: they were dancing the Ghost Dance.

The massacre at Wounded Knee and the Ghost Dance represent the unofficial end of the history of America's westward expansion and the long series of wars fought by Native Americans against the invaders. It is the symbolic last battle, although it was no battle. Perhaps more fittingly, it was the last act of the American Apocalypse. Wounded Knee was the final sanctioned murder of Indigenous people, apparent proof to the settlers that a Native spiritual vision was helpless against their own superior firepower and superior religious insight. The Ghost Dance seemed to die in the snow, ending generations of Native American prophets.

And yet the message of those prophets continued. In 1973 it was the memory of the Ghost Dancers that brought Native people back to Wounded Knee. It was the vision of Wovoka that inspired them and that, through them, inspired a whole new generation with the vision of Native American sovereignty and resistance. The martyrs at the first Wounded Knee led to the martyrs of the second Wounded Knee. The continuity of the vision was unbroken. The power of the dance could still be felt. It called to me just as it did to thousands of others of my culture. It called us to believe in an apocalyptic hope that could not die.

In 1924, the silent screen Western actor Tim McCoy invited Wovoka, the prophet of the Ghost Dance, to come out of seclusion to visit the outdoor set of his latest motion picture. Wovoka came, riding in a limousine provided by the star, and he spent time with the Native people who were extras in the movie, Arapahos who knew of the prophet and still revered him for his vision. "The last words

Wovoka said to me," McCoy wrote in his autobiography, "were the first he had uttered in English. As he climbed into the limousine and settled into his seat for the long ride back to Yerrington (Nevada), he looked out the window at me. Then he rolled the window down, stuck his hand out into the air, dropped a cake of red paint into my coat pocket and whispered, 'I will never die.'"

From the vantage point of a Native American and seeing how far and how long Wovoka's shadow has lain across our history, I believe I understand what he meant. In a very real sense, Wovoka has not died. His vision lives on, both consciously and subconsciously, in generations of Indigenous people. His myth remains powerful, his medicine strong. Something in Wovoka's vision touched more Native communities than any other Indigenous prophet did. His message transcended more boundaries than even Tenskwatawa was able to do. He drew scores of nations into his message, not with a political agenda but a spiritual one. And he did so without ever leaving his camp in a remote area of Nevada.

Once Wovoka's vision began to be shared, Native people from throughout the American West began sending delegations into the desert to find him. They came to see his miracles. They came to hear his vision. But most of all they came to learn his dance: the apocalyptic dance that came to be known as the Ghost Dance.

— • —

Wovoka was born into the Northern Paiute nation some-time around 1856. The area where he grew up was Mason Valley, Nevada; he rarely left it until later in life when he became a subject of curiosity. His father, Tavibo, was a recognized spiritual leader in the local community. Around 1869 Tavibo helped Wodziwob, a Dreamer prophet, to share an apocalyptic vision with the Paiute people.

Wodziwob, like so many Native prophets, had made the spirit journey to heaven and returned with a message of revitalization for the Native people. In 1860, the Paiute people had suffered a major defeat in a battle with the Americans at Pyramid Lake. Wodziwob's vision was very healing for them. It was a vision of long-lost family members in heaven. These ancestors (the "ghosts" of the Ghost Dance) would be reunited with their loved ones and the whole earth would be renewed when the living and the dead were joined in a promise of eternal life. Wodziwob introduced a dance and new songs to embody his vision and hasten the coming of the ancestor. But he died in 1872, and his local success soon faded.

Wovoka was to revive this vision and go on to not only complete his father's support for it but extend it far beyond the boundaries of the Paiute people. After Tavibo died when Wovoka was around fourteen years old, Wovoka found work with a white rancher in the valley named David Wilson. Wilson and his wife became like a second family for the young Wovoka, so much so that he also adopted the name Jack Wilson to show his kinship with them. Wovoka continued to live a life of simplicity in the Paiute way. He lived in the traditional wikiup, a cone-shaped shelter made of bent saplings and covered with mats of grass or reeds, sleeping on the ground. He never ventured far from his valley in Nevada.

Then, at the age of thirty, something strange happened to him. On January 1, 1889, Wovoka was out cutting wood when he heard a loud sound near the top of a hill. Curious to know what the sound might be, he began to walk up the hill when he suddenly fell to the ground unconscious. It was at the same moment as a solar eclipse. One observer described it this way:

On this occasion "the sun died" and he fell asleep in the daytime and was taken up to the other world. Here he saw God, with all the people who had died long ago engaged in their oldtime sport and occupations, all happy and forever young. It was a pleasant land and full of game. After showing him all, God told him he must go back and tell his people they must be good and love one another, have no quarreling, and live in peace with the whites; that they must work, and not lie or steal; that they must put away all the old practices that savored of war; that if they faithfully obeyed his instructions they would at last be reunited with their friends in this other world, where there would be no more death or sickness or old age. He was then given the dance which he was commanded to bring back to his people. By performing this dance at intervals, for five consecutive days each time, they would secure this happiness to themselves and hasten the event. Finally, God gave him control over the elements so that he could make it rain or snow or be dry at will.

As news of this vision spread among the Paiute people, small delegations from local communities made the pilgrimage to Wovoka's isolated valley to learn the new dance. Among the most unusual things about the dance is that it incorporated no use of the drum. First the people would prepare themselves by fasting and purification. They would enter the sweat lodge, cleansing themselves of all impurities, and then bathe in clear water. They would dress in traditional clothing, avoiding white people's clothing as much as possible. They would not wear any metal objects. Instead they would paint themselves with a red paint made from a natural ochre found in the desert—the same cake of dry red paint Wovoka slipped into the pocket of the Hollywood actor. They would use other colors as well, painting images sacred to them such as the thunderbird, eagles, buffalo, and the moon and stars.

These preparations would take most of a morning. Then the dance would begin when a young girl, standing in the center of the circle, would fire four arrows (with stone arrowheads, never metal) toward the four sacred directions. In some communities a large pole would be erected, a "tree of life" symbol, but in other cultures the dance ground would be unadorned.

Without the drum, the dance would begin with all the participants seated in a circle. A chant would be sung by a lead singer. Then food would be passed around the circle, a kind of simple communion to draw the dancers together in a spiritual act of sharing. Then on a signal from the leader of the dance, the people would rise, join hands, and begin to chant as they stepped from right to left, circling the dance grounds as they sang.

Here is a translation of one Ghost Dance song to give a sense of what the dancers were envisioning:

The whole world is coming,
A nation is coming, a nation is coming,
The Eagle has brought a message to the tribe.
The father says so, the father says so.
Over the whole earth they are coming.
The buffalo are coming, the buffalo are coming.
The Crow has brought the message to the tribe,
The father says so, the father says so.

This simple and stately dance was the core of the Ghost Dance. By performing it, people hoped to hasten the coming of Wovoka's apocalyptic vision. They sought to reunite themselves with their ancestors, restoring the earth to the fullness of its bounty and resurrecting the ancient values of the Indigenous culture. As news of this dance spread, more delegations of Native people made the long trek to Wovoka's desert valley. They came from over thirty Native nations, including the Cheyenne, Shoshone, Caddo, Kiowa, Lakota, and Arapaho.

Each delegation brought its skeptics along with its true believers, for not every Native person who encountered Wovoka believed in his vision. But a great many did, and within a year his Ghost Dance was being carried out from North Dakota to New Mexico. Wovoka's dream had touched a spiritual nerve among the beleaguered people of the Plains. As the pilgrims returned home from their meeting with the prophet, they brought his universal vision to their cultural reality. The mixture of the two began to produce hybrids of the original Ghost Dance, especially among the Lakota.

Wovoka had never described any special clothing for his dance, aside from a prohibition against Western-style clothing and metal objects, but among the Cheyenne and Lakota a new phenomenon arose: the ghost shirt. It was said to make whoever wore it invulnerable to the bullets of the American invaders. This idea was taken up primarily by younger men who sought to use the Ghost Dance as a show of resistance to further white incursions. They would fashion traditional fringed buckskin shirts with images of sacred animals or stars on them. They believed these special shirts could protect them from harm.

Remember that by this time the Native communities of the Northern plains were becoming desperate. The apocalypse they faced came crashing down on them by the terms of the Fort Laramie Treaty of 1868. Once gold was discovered in the Black Hills, the federal government threw away its solemn treaty promising the Lakota their ancestral lands in North and South Dakota. Almost eleven million acres of their lands were stolen from them. The buffalo, on whom they had relied as their primary food source, had been systematically exterminated as a tactic of war by the American military. Confined to local reservations, they existed on the handouts of food subsidies from their conquerors. If those supplies failed to arrive on time, they faced starvation.

Consequently, in nations that were literally struggling to survive, the Ghost Dance became more intense. Like Pentecostal Christians, some Ghost Dancers would enter a trance state. Some would faint or cry out. The young men would wear their ghost shirts and shout their defiance against the evil that was slowly killing their people. It was from this elaboration on the original dance that the path to the massacre at Wounded Knee began.

American agents and military commanders began hearing of the Ghost Dance. While it was an apocalyptic vision of renewal, those within Western culture saw it as a frenzied war dance designed to prepare the Native people for battle. Rumors about the dance spread quickly through white communities. Settlers, miners, and railroad workers became alarmed. Without any real understanding of the dance or its meaning, they assumed anything that could revive Native people from their oppression must be dangerous. They demanded protection from the army. They insisted that the Ghost Dance be suppressed and its leaders arrested.

— • —

One such leader was Sitting Bull (Tata'nka I'yota'nke). His name and reputation are among the best known of Indigenous leaders in American history. He is often described as the "chief" of the Lakota people, but he was, in fact, a spiritual leader, a medicine person of great stature for his integrity and courage. In 1890, one of the two main sites of the Ghost Dance in the Dakotas was on his land. He encouraged his people to take up the dance as a way to appeal to the Great Spirit to bring justice to the oppressed.

By December of that year, the American authorities were sufficiently afraid of the dance to plan the arrest of Sitting Bull. A number of "Indian police," backed up by a company of American troops, descended on Sitting Bull's home to make the arrest. As so often happens in volatile situations like this, things got out of control. Members of Sitting Bull's family protested. Some of the women ran forward to protect him. A shoving match began and then gunfire.

Sitting Bull was killed on December 15, 1890, at about fifty-six years of age. He died because of the Ghost Dance, which he understood to be a sacred liturgy of hope and reconciliation, but which his killers took to be a war dance by "Indian hostiles." Ignoring the Constitution, the American government proclaimed the Ghost Dance religion to be outlawed. Without ever seeing or understanding it, they simply made it illegal. This level of paranoia on the part of the dominant culture led, a short time later, to the infamous massacre at Wounded Knee on the Pine Ridge reservation. So great was the Americans' fear that even a small band of starving people were seen as dangerous—so dangerous they had to be wiped out.

The massacre of unarmed dancers, the women and children left in the snow, had a chilling effect on all the nations that had taken up the dance. Among most of them there were no ghost shirts or trances. The dances were the simple but dignified invocations of a people facing an apocalypse.

The level of brutality associated with Wounded Knee shocked the Indigenous nations and caused them to take the dance underground. To spare the lives of the innocent, Wovoka called on people to stop dancing in 1892. But the dances continued in secret for many years.

— • —

Why? Why would people continue to risk their lives over a dance? That is the question that reveals the true apocalyptic nature of Wovoka's prophecy. When apocalypse as event (Wounded Knee) meets apocalypse as revelation (the Ghost Dance), the result is a spiritual catharsis. The apocalyptic process comes full circle.

The apocalyptic process begins with a reality: the invasion of Native land by a foreign culture. That event leads to a revelation: Wovoka's vision of a new heaven and new earth. That vision prompts a reaction: the massacre at Wounded Knee. That tragedy makes the next revelation (the Ghost Dance) even more urgent. The process begins spinning out of control until it buries itself underground in the hidden dimensions of racial prejudice and trauma.

Fear is the source of the Ghost Dance. Fear is also the source of the reaction against it. The emotional context of any apocalypse, either as event or revelation, is fear. We either see something fearful coming our way or we are in the midst of experiencing it: either way, the core emotion is the same.

In the brief time it flourished, the Ghost Dance religion spread rapidly among Native people who spoke different languages and practiced different cultures. It spread person by person as pilgrims made the long journey into the Nevada desert to find the prophet. Wovoka never left his home. He would welcome people to his camp, tell them his vision, and then invite them to join the dance. Given the distance, time, and expense of travel in that era, it is remarkable how quickly the new religion took root. I believe it did so because the motivation of its followers was so driven by fear of genocide.

By the 1890s, the Native nations in the Central and Northern plains were the last of the historical dominos to fall to Manifest Destiny. Native people like the Cheyenne and Lakota had seen what happened to the Native people of the eastern and western coasts of America. They had experienced the American Apocalypse firsthand. They had struggled against the overwhelming force of American military power and lost. They had been confined to fragments of land and forced to live on handouts. Their children had been taken from them and forced into re-education centers called boarding schools. Their fear was not ungrounded. The newspapers of the day were already describing them as the "vanishing Americans."

Wovoka's vision gave these Indigenous communities the one thing people living in a state of fear need the most: hope. His message was simple, and it was the classic reply of apocalyptic revelation. One day things will change. They will get better. In fact, divine intervention will do what people are not able to do for themselves. They will be rescued. Their lands will be restored, their families reunited, their traditions will be revitalized.

This central vision offers desperate people what they long to see, a way out of fear into belief in a future. The Ghost Dance gave Native people a sense of future. It said that they would survive the physical apocalypse they had been experiencing. It promised that one day soon they would be vindicated and redeemed. The last would become the first.

Ironically, that hope became the fear for the dominant culture. Fear of the Ghost Dance spread almost as quickly as hope in the dance. From ground zero in Nevada the fear radiated out, becoming more virulent the farther out it went. In the local region around Wovoka's camp, the white community was not as alarmed. They knew the man they called Jack Wilson. They were aware of how vulnerable the local Native community was by this time in history. But the more news of the Ghost Dance religion expanded into other white communities, the more fearful its image became.

Even though they had no idea what the dance symbolized, much less seen it for themselves, the mere thought of a Native American revival sent shock waves through the newspapers, government offices, and military forts of the dominant culture. A level of hysteria emerged. Telegraph messages flew around the country from frightened schoolteachers and ranchers, predicting an imminent attack by thousands of Ghost Dance fanatics. Territorial governors issued a call for more troops. Fear outran reason, and white settlers began to see ghosts around every corner. Their fear was irrational, since at this late date the ability of any Native American community to sustain a military campaign was reduced to the level of Geronimo's heroic single-handed resistance, but it was still fear—fear so real that it led to the massacre at Wounded Knee.

The Ghost Dance reveals the fault lines of fear running through the history of Native American prophets. Wovoka and his peers were reacting spiritually to the fear they felt around them. They arose from communities living in the fear of an apocalypse, either one they had endured already or were anticipating at any moment. They knew their fears were genuine. They had seen the evidence all around them. The last effort to pull fearful people back from the abyss of despair was an apocalyptic revelation, a hope that things could change for the better.

Prophets are hope givers. They are fear healers. Wovoka's prophecy—of a return of the buffalo and the ancestors—was a small whisper after the massive collapse of traditional Native American civilization at the end of the nineteenth century, but for people starved of hope, literally, it was a shout of liberation—perhaps the last hope for a weary nation.

And yet, while the Ghost Dance revealed the hope of the Indigenous people, it also revealed the fear of the white community. A deep-seated fear, one not of conflict but of exposure. The desperate dance of the Indigenous people pulled back the curtain on American colonialism. It exposed the truth of the powers driving Western expansion: racism, greed, genocide. This was not the reflection Americans wanted to see in the mirror of history. Somewhere in the subconscious mind of the invaders was a recognition, a mea culpa, that they had been doing more than just following orders. That shame and culpability had to be reduced to a whisper through denial and misinformation. Therefore, the abused had to be labeled the abuser. The threat had to be seen coming from the victims so the perpetrators could remain hidden. Fear of exposure—of their own culpability—was a more likely reason for Wounded Knee rather than fear of a few hungry women and their babies.

One of the primary issues a study of the apocalyptic prophets of Native America demonstrates for us is the role of fear as a subtext for apocalypse, both real and imagined. The spread of disinformation, the intentional rewriting of history, the scapegoating, the transference of blame: all of these are dynamic forces at work beneath the surface of what we see. They are the hidden agenda we can never seem to isolate and expose clearly.

To talk about the way fear operates within cultures is uncomfortable, painful, and even dangerous. Yet if we want to avoid repeating history, it is a challenge we must accept. To reconcile the emotional apartheid of colonialism, we must find a sliver of common ground on which both the abused and the abuser may stand together in the full light of truth and justice. Other prophetic voices than Native America—voices like Mahatma Gandhi and Nelson Mandela—have called us to this apocalyptic process before. They have demonstrated that reconciliation must be transparent and factual. Without those conditions in place, the relationship between cultures is reduced to rumor and subverted by fear.

The Ghost Dance religion was a vision Native Americans could embrace at the close of a long and bloody history because it acknowledged the truth of their situation. It was a vision white settlers feared because it exposed that truth for all the world to see. As long as Indigenous people were seen as wild, savage, and dangerous, the colonial myth could be maintained. Once these same people were seen as vulnerable human beings, no different in their aspirations from any other culture or community, the myth would collapse. Even more importantly, the question of accountability and responsibility would be surfaced. It might be fair to say that an enormous effort has been made in American history to keep that from happening. For generations no sliver of common ground between the two cultures could be found because the fear of exposure outweighed the desire for historical integrity.

— • —

So does fear have the last word in the story of the Ghost Dance? No, hope does, and for a reason. When Wovoka revealed his original vision, he did so in his own Paiute language. When pilgrims came from scores of different nations to learn this vision, they did so through interpreters. When he spoke to white people about it, he did so with a marginal command of English. Could something have been lost in translation? The process of transmission of his vision through different languages becomes important in terms of one key aspect of his vision.

According to some interpreters, Wovoka saw only Native American ancestors in his view of heaven, but according to others, he saw white people as well. In fact, the implication is that he saw people of all races and cultures gathered into a heavenly community. His vision was one of diversity and equality. As one historian has put it, if this is true, "Wovoka's religion was all the more remarkable insofar as it projected a racially integrated life to come." Given the levels of fear on both sides of the Ghost Dance, this quiet possibility of reconciliation seems even more profound. The first white interviewers to reach Wovoka reported clearly that his teaching was that "all believers were exhorted to make themselves worthy of the predicted happiness by discarding all things warlike and practicing honesty, peace, and good will, not only among themselves, but also toward the whites, so long as they were together."

Did some Native American followers hope they would not be together with whites for long, but taken up in a kind of rapture of the Indigenous people? Probably. But did others understand the message that all people must share in the apocalyptic renewal of human life together? Yes, undoubtedly.

And from that possibility—the simple recognition of our common humanity—emerges the hope that inspired so many people to invest themselves, even to the cost of their own lives, in the message Wovoka brought to them. Like all religious messages, Wovoka's vision is open to inter- pretation, including revision. The nations of the Southern plains who followed Wovoka and had made the trip to Nevada to meet with him did not hear a call in his words to make a ghost shirt that was bullet proof. Some North- ern plains people did. Some Ghost Dancers erected a tree of life at the center of the dance grounds; others did not. Some experienced ecstatic trances; others did not. But the core message—the vision of a renewal and reconciliation for all life—remained at the center of what motivated hope in the hearts of Native people from across the wide spectrum of languages and cultures. The essence of the vision was hope, not fear—and hope for all, not only for a few.

One of the fundamental lessons of the Ghost Dance was that a vision must spread not only widely but deeply. The apocalyptic hope of the dance was so strong that it reached deep into the struggling cultures of Native America. It was a spiritual taproot into the core of their survival. If all else failed, at least there was the hope that the Great Spirit would intervene and offer the miraculous salvation that Native people could not give to themselves. The dance sought to materialize the hope, conjuring it into reality through faith alone.

This led to the second critical lesson of the Ghost Dance after the slaughter at Wounded Knee: ghost shirts don't work. If we look for a meaning of the Ghost Dance for our own apocalyptic peril, it may be the same realization that came to Wovoka's followers: there is no magic that produces reconciliation—no good luck charm to protect us from harm. Just because we long for reconciliation and healing does not mean they will happen. In fact, reconciliation is a complicated, difficult, and dangerous undertaking.

Nothing can protect us from the fact that some people, out of their own prejudice and fear, will lash out when the truth is presented to them. They are not interested in halting the apocalypse because they have a vested interest in not doing so.

The bigotry and greed that dominated the relationship between Native Americans and white colonizers was institutionalized by the 1890s. It was endemic. It could not be easily identified, much less exposed because, like the Ghost Dance, it had put down deep roots in the American psyche. Justification for the false treaties, land grabs, child abuse, and oppression were buried deeply in the myth of Manifest Destiny. To unravel it publicly would be to expose the long record of pain and injustice of colonialism. Therefore, the reality had to be suppressed. Racism became entrenched in American history. Confronting it would require more than a magic shirt.

— • —

To reach a place of genuine reconciliation—between races, between political opinions, between people and planet—will require a level of truth telling and truth receiving that will only provoke a reaction of fear from those who believe themselves in positions of power. The experience of post-apartheid South Africa in its truth and reconciliation process is a model for apocalyptic revelation: an uncovering of what has been hidden.

Sitting Bull was killed outside his own home on his own land for the crime of dancing. Like his peers, he was dancing to hurry Wovoka's vision into being—a vision that clearly embodied a hope for reconciliation and a willingness to coexist, even if doing so was difficult. As long as white people and Native people were together, according to the vision, they must live in mutual respect and peace. The message was clear, but its intent did not matter to those who felt threatened by its implications. Equality is an aspiration for some but a threat to others.

There are no shortcuts to reconciliation. No quick fixes. No magic. Only honesty and hard work, facts and figures, accountability and responsibility, justice and acts of restoration. The process of reconciliation, which can prevent an apocalypse, requires a level of commitment as intense as that of the Ghost Dancers. The degree to which we believe in a future of equality, sharing, and cooperation will determine the degree to which we are willing to remain engaged in the process of reconciliation. It will test how deep our own faith is when confronted with anger, denial, and misinformation. The women and children at Wounded Knee were unarmed. We will be too.

Wovoka's challenge to us is to believe that the miraculous can happen even without the miracle. If only we keep dancing. If only we keep believing. And if only we keep showing up to do the work that must be done. We will not have a ghost shirt to protect us any more than we will be safe behind our own sense of right and wrong. The power of apocalypse can appear invincible, and its response to our intentions can be violent and irrational. That is the simple truth on the Ghost Dance grounds. There is no escaping the accumulated history of colonialism that had brought us, willingly or not, to this place in our shared history. We cannot avoid the pain of reconciliation, if reconciliation is to be more than historic window dressing.

The roots of fear run deep. The hope we embrace must run just as deep. No matter what happens we must keep dancing, hand in hand, joined in a circle of equality, constantly moving in the slow rotation of justice and prayer. Like Wovoka's dancers, we must be dedicated to a vision and willing to dance for it for as long as it takes. That level of commitment is not common in our age, but it is what will be necessary if we are to diminish the apocalypse we see rising before us. Not magic, but faith is what will see us through.

As a Native American I am so struck by the fact that this dance, unlike any other, must take place without the drum. The use of the drum as a ubiquitous presence in our traditional worship leaves me wondering what it must have been like to dance without it, without that comforting heartbeat of the earth that formed the cadence for our movement as a people through time and space. The silence it leaves at the center of the Ghost Dance seems eerie to me, like stepping out into the emptiness of space.

Yet I have come to appreciate Wovoka more because of that silence. Without the drum, all I have is the physical sensation of being joined to my brothers and sisters in an endless circle. All I hear is our combined voice rising into the thin air in a lament and expectation. We are weightless and floating. Nothing grounds us but our own faith that someone out there is listening, and more important, someone who cares.

Wovoka's dance reminds me that there are times in life when we must have the willingness to go beyond what we think is possible. We have never encountered a world like this before; how will we survive it, much less transform it? The silent drum forces me to recognize that in this dance we are moving into uncharted territory. We are stepping off the familiar into the unknown. We are creating a dance ground where none has existed before. The willingness, the faith, to take such a step is the haunting silence of the Ghost Dance.

Wovoka himself fell silent on January 29, 1932. He died in his cabin in the same valley he had called home all of his life. He was seventy-four years of age. He was buried beside his wife of fifty years. His death would seem to make false his strange statement to movie star Tim McCoy, "I will never die."

Wovoka had never recanted his vision, even after the tragedy of Wounded Knee made his religion go underground. He kept the faith, and so did many others. When he made his visit to the set of McCoy's movie in 1924, he was surrounded by Native people who sought his blessing. They had not forgotten him or his invitation to dance in silence. Through all those years Wovoka had remained in his out-of-the-way world in rural Nevada. He never denied his original vision, including the part that said he would have control over the elements. Local Paiutes and white ranchers had claimed to witness his amazing ability to bring rain or snow, but most of the white media only used these claims as vehicles of ridicule for the old Indian living in his isolated valley.

Wovoka had told his people that when he finally went to heaven, he would send back a sign to his followers that he still lived and his vision was true. Three months to the day of his passing, December 23, 1932, the local *Mason Valley News* reported the most severe earthquake the area had ever known. The epicenter was Wovoka's home.

6

THE HOPI
Migrating through Time and Space

*That these Hopis have revealed their conceptual pattern
of life to us now, for the first time, imparts to their gift a
strangeness unique in our national experience. For they
speak not as a defeated little minority in the richest and
most powerful nation on earth, but with the voice of all that
world commonwealth of peoples who affirm their right to grow
from their own native roots. They evoke old gods shaped by
instincts we have long repressed. They reassert a rhythm of life
we have disastrously tried to ignore. They remind us we must
attune ourselves to the need for inner change if we are to avert
a cataclysmic rupture between our own minds and hearts.
Now, if ever, is the time for them to talk, for us to listen.*

—Frank Waters

WE ARE LIVING in the Fourth World. Soon, if the
prophecies are correct, and they have been so far for

---

generations, we will enter an apocalypse of transformation that will close the chapter on this age and lead to our emergence into the Fifth World.

This is the spiritual vision of the Hopi, a small Native American community living in present-day Arizona. The Hopi are not founders of a great confederacy of Indigenous nations like the Seneca of Ganiodaiio, or a warrior nation like the Shawnee of Tenskwatawa, or a people skilled at diplomacy like the Wanapams of Smohalla, or a people who inspired a national upheaval like the Paiute of Wovoka. Their name, Hopi, means the Peaceful Ones, and that is what they have been, living in the deserts of the American Southwest for more generations than people can count. By their own reckoning through myth and symbol, their memory may go back to the end of the Ice Age or to the island-hopping voyages across the Pacific Ocean that brought them to the shores of California.

The Hopi are a people of mystery both by the endless depths of their story, still being deciphered by anthropologists and archeologists, and by their own intentional secretiveness, a reaction born of many past abuses of their people by outsiders. As a small community, living on mesa tops in a challenging desert environment, they have been surrounded by other Native peoples like the Navajo, invaded by oppressive cultures like the Spanish conquistadores, and dominated by the controlling intrusion of the

United States. In each instance the Hopi have resisted, struggling to maintain the integrity of their own history and spirituality.

The Hopi sought a peaceful accommodation with the Spanish in the sixteenth century, but they fought back when the Spanish tried to convert them to Catholicism. They sought a peaceful resolution with the Americans in the nineteenth century, but they fought back when the Americans tried to convert them to Protestantism. In many ways they were the forerunners of the nonviolent resistance embodied in leaders like Mahatma Gandhi and Martin Luther King Jr. When the American government sought to kidnap their children to force them into English-speaking-only schools, Hopi fathers who resisted were arrested and sent to prison on Alcatraz Island. In retribution, Hopi land was taken, many of their traditional sacred sites were violated or destroyed, and their self-governance was denied them. In short, the Hopi have suffered the American Apocalypse for centuries, but they have survived.

How? How did such a small community survive so many assaults over such a long period of time? The reason is etched on the canyon walls of their desert home for anyone to see. Throughout the Southwest are petroglyphs: signs and symbols carved on the rocks that tell a religious story so old that the meanings have been lost to time. Except to the Hopi. These images, such as people, animals, spirals, and celestial events, still have a meaning for the Hopi. They contain a sacred narrative. Like the pages of Scripture written on rock, they tell of the long migration stories, the exodus account of the Hopi ancestors across the landscape over hundreds of generations. They indicate that the Hopi not only resided in different places throughout the region but that they traveled extensively, establishing communities in many different locations, only to leave and resume their wanderings again.

By Hopi reckoning, the phenomenal cliff dwellings of places like Mesa Verde are part of that epic story, as are Chaco Canyon and the Grand Canyon. On almost any piece of land in the Southwest you may uncover broken pieces of ancient pottery: proof to the Hopi of the passing of their ancestors on the long cycle of their travels through the centuries. In long-abandoned settlements, places reduced to rubble through the erosion of the mud bricks used to create them, the outlines of ancient kivas, underground ceremonial spaces, can still be discerned. According to the Hopi those kivas validate the continuity of Hopi religion over a vast stretch of time. They even see their handprint on the building of the mounds through much of the heartland of North America, including the Great Serpent Mound in Ohio. They believe this is an effigy of one of their many clans, the serpent clan. The Hopi may have been endlessly moving over the landscape, but they took their faith with them. Like the Hebrew people under Moses, they wandered the desert taking their sense of themselves as the people of God wherever they went.

It is the history of their migrations that the Hopi wrote on the walls of their desert world. It was their record of what sent them on their trek over the continent. The secret to their survival can be found in this story of their creation. The Hopi believe they were created for a purpose, one that they have sought to fulfill through time immemorial. Surviving not only one apocalypse, but many apocalypses, they have done so by migrating across time and space.

— • —

We are living in the Fourth World. Three worlds before us have emerged, flourished, and then collapsed. The Hopi have lived through two of them: the end of the world by flood and by an ice age. The Hopi can look back to see the human story from its first steps on the evolutionary journey to its current condition in an age of technology. The reason they resist conversion from their faith is because without the Hopi we would, as the human race, lose our memory. We would become victims of spiritual amnesia and fail to remember why we are here. The result would be catastrophic—an apocalypse from which we might not recover.

The Hopi know why we are here. They have known from the beginning. For centuries, on the open plazas of their villages or within the flickering light of their underground kivas, they have carried out the ceremonies and rituals that keep the memory alive. Through their religious devotion, they maintain the harmony and balance of creation. They keep an equilibrium between people and planet. They hold up the light of wisdom and humility that are essential to human survival.

The Hopi are the memory keepers for humanity, the line of our unbroken continuity with the creation, the story of our long migration through time and space. Therefore, the Hopi prophetic tradition is not a doomsday depiction of future cataclysms but a projection of profound hope into the future. Their faith is grounded in a pragmatic optimism. One outside observer writes,

> These important prophecies tell us in advance what we should anticipate and prepare for, teaching us caution and awareness. They tell us why things will happen, thus helping us understand ourselves, the nature of the world, and the nature of our Creator. We are not left to sit, to wonder, or to live in fear. . . . In Hopi prophecy life functions as a global play in which all of us are the actors. There are possible things that can happen in each act, but we ourselves determine which of these it will be by what we choose to do. The traditional Hopi believe we

are in the midst of the final act today, as the Fourth Cycle of the world closes down, and we can shape and reshape its form if we make the right choices. In Hopi prophecy, there are no fated endings set in concrete.

My task in this book is not to pretend to reveal all the meanings or secrets of the Hopi prophecy. In fact, it is not my desire to steal anyone's spiritual knowledge. It is for the Hopi to share their own teachings if and when they choose to do so, and in the manner they choose. I respect their decision because it is based on so many experiences of betrayal and oppression. It is enough for me to walk behind them, on the well-worn path they have made through their homeland, and stand beside them before the writing on the wall.

All those ancient signs and symbols, all those recorded memories, all those invitations to a deeper understanding: let's allow the petroglyphs to speak for themselves. We can be silent and listen.

— • —

What I hear is an echo. The Hopi knowledge that is public reminds me of something. The creation story of the Hopi, and the migration stories that followed that point of origin, reverberate through Native American spiritual history. They embody themes that appear elsewhere among Native people, including among my own people, Chahta Yakni, or the Choctaw Nation.

The Hopi provide a context for the four prophets. Their authenticity is established by their fulfillment of a shared faith that runs through North America's Indigenous nations. They have an explanation for why Native American nations share the same prophetic traditions. They tie the four prophets together in offering each of them a common point of origin.

Emergence is the genesis point for all Native cultures. It is the creation cycle that carried human beings through layers of realities, helping us to emerge from the apocalypses of each new world. The Hopi prophecy, therefore, is not an isolated and curious artifact from a small and esoteric community. Instead, the cosmic nature of Hopi prophecy seems suddenly clear in its resonance with other nations, in other times, far removed from the ancient cliff dwellings.

In its universality, the Hopi experience becomes foundational. It is both the memory of a particular people and the intuition of many more. The echo is there among the Seneca, the Shawnee, the Wanapams, and the Paiutes. What the Hopi prophesied came true for the choices made by Ganiodaiio, Tenskwatawa, Smohalla, and Wovoka. Like me, like all of us, they were actors in the universal drama of the Hopi's sacred narrative. What the four prophets taught can be found in the Hopi testament as well, placed there

perhaps centuries before their time on earth. The petroglyphs left by Hopi ancestors record more than the journeys of a special people; they also point to the emergence
of a broader wisdom among all the Native people of North
America. They draw the messages of the prophets we have
encountered into a wider context.

— • —

The Hopi creation story sets the stage for this global play
with a breathtaking sophistication. In the First World there
was only Tokpela, endless space. In this void was a single
consciousness, Tawa, the Creator. Tawa considered the
emptiness of space and had a thought. Creation, therefore, began not with a word but with an idea. The thought
precedes the word as the idea precedes the action. The
origin of the universe was this "big bang" moment of an
inspiration in a mind of infinite scope and power.

Tawa's idea was to fill the void, but to do so would require
the presence of matter and energy. These two elements were
the necessary agents of creation. Tawa created them by willing into being Sotuknang, a being of pure matter with the
capability of pure energy. Under Tawa's authority, Sotuknang
shaped matter and energy into a series of universes, some
to exist now and some to become future realities. What we
would now call the multiverse came into existence.

Tawa, who is pure thought, was pleased with this physical creation but then had another idea: life. Tawa instructed Sotuknang, matter and energy, to form life in the First World. This assignment was a new level of intricacy, so Sotuknang willed into being a spirit of life, the essence of evolution, Gogyeng Sowuthi, Spider Grandmother. She took matter in the form of clay and shaped two dolls from it. She covered the dolls with a cloth and sang the Creation Song over them. When she removed the cloth a living pair of twins emerged, Pokanghoya and Polongahoya, whose first words were, "Who are we? Why are we here?"

Those two simple questions are at the heart of Hopi religion. They are the primal questions that set the creation of human life into motion and that follow humanity throughout our journey in time and space. To remember the answers, on behalf of us all, is the core of Hopi faith. To forget them is the source of apocalypse.

Part of the sophistication of Hopi theology is that it is not rooted in laws or creeds that must be adhered to, as if humanity already had the answers to all its questions. Instead, Hopi theology is framed in the realm of human curiosity, our endless quest for knowledge and understanding. In the Hopi vision, when we stop being able to ask questions, we stop being human.

The Twins, Pokanghoya and Polongahoya, were sent around the world, which the Hopi already knew to be round, creating the conditions for life; then they took up their positions at the North and South Poles, and by generating a powerful vibration, they spun the ball of the Earth and kept it in alignment with its axis. It is helpful to remember that this was the Hopi vision of reality in the same era in which Europeans still believed the planet was flat and if you sailed too far west, you would fall off the edge.

The first echo I hear from the four prophets is here: in the resonance between Ganiodaiio and the primal questions at the source of Hopi tradition. Ganiodaiio taught a practice of deep introspection on who we are as human beings. Why are we here? What are we to do? What is our relationship to others? These are the questions that lead out of apocalypse into a life of balance and meaning. That is what the Gaiwiio of the Seneca prophet sought to maintain. And it did so by making people think for themselves. By intentionally focusing on the responsibility of the individual to be in harmony with the needs of the community, Ganiodaiio was unknowingly in tune with the ancient Hopi vision. Unless this kind of introspection is practiced over and over again, people will lose their focus, forget their purpose, and wander into chaos.

To question is to believe, to believe is to question: this psychological and spiritual dynamic is at the center of the Gaiwiio, just as it is in Hopi tradition. After creating the

Twins, Spider Grandmother continued her work of generating life. She formed the first human beings from four colors of clay: red, white, black, yellow. Human life, therefore, begins in a recognition of sacred diversity, but diversity with a single purpose. She explained to the first humans that their purpose was to sing praises to their Creator and to keep asking the questions that would lead them to understand their deeper purpose in life. As one scholar wrote,

> The road to the Upper World was finished, and the people rested. Spider Grandmother spoke, telling of things to come. She said: the journey will be long and difficult. When we reach the Upper World, that will only be the beginning. Things there are not like things here. You will discover new ways of doing things. During the journey you must try to discover the meaning of life and learn to distinguish between good and evil. Tawa did not intend for you to live in the midst of chaos and dissent. In the Upper World you must learn to be true humans.

Ganiodaiio wanted the Seneca to become true human beings, not victims of history, by focusing on their inner strength and faith in the Creator. To do this he challenged them to make a deep "adjustment" to their cultural thinking. In the same way Hopi tradition tells us, in the words of one author, "that human beings the world over must undergo a total change in attitude regarding life." We must not lose our memory. We must avoid the spiritual amnesia that physical comfort and material wealth create in our minds. Instead, we must continue the journey of discovery, always asking Tawa to show us the higher purpose to our being. The Gaiwiio and the Hopi are in alignment as the creation story begins.

— • —

After the First World, the story continues. The Hopi see geological history as spiritual history. At the end of the First World comes an apocalypse by fire. Great volcanic explosions occur that destroy life, but that also set the stage for act two of the global play.

To preserve human beings, Spider Grandmother leads them down into the earth to seek shelter with the Ant People. These industrious beings keep the humans fed until it is time to emerge into the Second World, Tokpa. In fact, the reason ants have such tiny stomachs is because they gave most of their food to the humans they sheltered during the apocalypse that ended the First World.

This salvation of humanity brings us to the second echo we hear from the Native American prophets: the importance of sacred space as envisioned by Tenskwatawa of the Shawnee.

As the dust and ash from the volcanoes subsides, Sotuknang addresses the human family:

"You will go to a certain place. Your ko'pavi will lead you. This inner wisdom will give you the sight to see a certain cloud, which you will follow by day, and a certain star, which you will follow by night. Take nothing with you. Your journey will not end until the cloud stops and the star stops." After many days and nights the first people arrived at the certain place. They were all happy together because they were of the same mind and understanding even though they were of different races and languages.

Where is your certain place? Hopi cosmology asks that question and so did Tenskwatawa. The Shawnee prophet wanted to establish a sacred space, a tangible focal point for the faith of Native American people, people who were different from one another but who would occupy the same ground. Otherwise, they would be uprooted and vulnerable nations, easily overcome by superior numbers and firepower. They would be susceptible to an apocalypse. But if they had a rock on which to stand, a physical center to their faith, then they would be able to withstand any adversity.

The importance of this place is not that it was a physical shelter alone, like the mythical refuge of the Ant People, but because it embodied a shared wisdom—the "inner wisdom" that all human beings possess, if they will only remember to use it. And that wisdom is located in the ko'pavi, the vibrational center at the top of the head.

Like the chakras of Hindu philosophy, the Hopi identified "certain places" in the inner body just as they saw them in geographic locations of the natural world. The first sacred place in the body was the ko'pavi at the top of the head, then the brain, the throat, the heart, and the solar plexus. Each of these was a vibrational point, in tune with the energy fields sent out by the Twins to keep creation balanced. By accessing the ko'pavi, people could find their sense of place and grow stronger in spiritual wisdom.

And what was the meaning of the ko'pavi? In Hopi the word means "the open door." And what was the meaning of Tenskwatawa? In Shawnee the name means "the open door." Tenskwatawa sought to bring all the nations between the Appalachians and the Mississippi together into one place, physically symbolized by Prophetstown but spiritually resident in every Native American heart. He sought to help Native people see they had the same vision even though they were of different cultures and languages. The Hopi tradition and the Shawnee prophet echo one another, and by so doing, they invite us to answer the question for ourselves: Where is our place in spiritual life? Where are we going? Where do we belong?

Searching for answers to those questions is why so much of the Hopi religion is based on the idea of a migration. As each successive "world" faces its apocalypse and gives way to another in Hopi tradition, so the human beings who are an integral part of it must keep moving to find their place. The search for the place of our belonging is crucial. Just as we keep asking questions, we also keep moving through the physical landscape of our lives. We grow. We change. We learn. Each step takes us to a different level of understanding—one that we can only achieve if (a) we are in the place where the Creator wants us to be, and (b) we are not alone in being there, but in the company of people who are different than we are. The implications of both Hopi teachings and the vision of Tenskwatawa is that, by definition, the holy place we are called to inhabit is a multicultural community.

— • —

Failure to create that kind of community led to the apocalypse that ended the Second World and opened the door to the Third World, Kuskurza—a word so old its exact meaning in Hopi has been lost. However, the way the Second World ended may give us a clue: it was a great ice age.

This natural apocalypse was brought on by the breakdown in multicultural community. Although the people had all that they needed in the Second World, some people wanted more. This desire to be set apart from others by race, power, or possessions was the fatal flaw in human beings. Instead of singing the praises of Tawa, instead of asking questions, and instead of coming together as one family, the people of the Second World began to spend their time gathering wealth and oppressing others. Consequently, the Second World died in an icy reality of hearts frozen by greed.

The Third World emerged and people continued their migrations until the coming of a great flood. Spider Grandmother fashioned reed boats and helped humanity survive this apocalypse. The Hopi remember long voyages on the sea, island hopping until they arrived on the shores of an unknown land. Sotuknang appeared to them there, telling them that this was Tu'waqachi, the Fourth World:

It has height and depth, heat and cold, beauty and barrenness; it has everything for you to choose from. What you choose will determine if this time you can carry out the plan of creation on it or whether it must in time be destroyed too. Now you will separate and go different ways to claim the earth for the Creator. Each group of you will follow your own star until it stops. There you will settle. Now I must go. Just keep your own doors open and always remember what I have told you.

The Fourth World is Tu'waqachi: the Complete World, the one we inhabit today. It is complete, because as Sotuknang says, it contains all we need to live in beauty and harmony. The choice is ours. We must all travel in this world and "claim" it for the Creator. But what does that mean? How do we choose to claim the gift that has been given to us, knowing that our answer can lead to either abundance or apocalypse?

Those questions have an echo in the voice of the prophet Smohalla. In his many appeals to the white colonizers to respect the land, Smohalla calls us to the choice between barrenness and beauty. His highly evocative language of Mother Earth embodies the vision of "claiming" the earth—not by right of ecological conquest, however, but by the relationship between two living beings.

The Hopi made the choice to envision their relationship to the Earth in an intimate way. It was not just utilitarian. It was personal. For example, like so many Native American nations, the Hopi depended on the staple crop of corn to sustain their communities. And like Ganiodaiio's vision in the cornfield, they felt the living presence of the Earth in the world around them. As Frank Waters has written,

> With the pristine wisdom granted them, they understood that the earth was a living entity like themselves. She was their mother; they were made from her flesh; they suckled at her breast. For her milk was the grass upon which

all animals grazed and the corn which had been created specially to supply food for mankind. But the corn was also a living entity with a body similar to man's in many respects, and the people built its flesh into their very own. Hence corn was also their mother. Thus they knew their mother in two aspects which were synonymous—as Mother Earth and Corn Mother.

What the Hopi understood in their primordial entrance into the Fourth World, our world, was a spiritual conviction shared by all the Indigenous nations that migrated across North America to find their place on the land. Claiming the land was not ownership, but relationship. The Mother claims us as her children. We claim the Mother as our parent. A sacred bond exists between us, a living bond of mutual care and respect.

As simple as this emotional equation seems, it appears to be extraordinarily difficult for some people to embrace. The generals who chased Chief Joseph to the Canadian border could not grasp it, nor could the missionaries who destroyed Hopi religious sites. For them, the earth remained inanimate. It was a vast pile of resources, nothing more. Consequently, the relationship was only a matter of convenience, not of love.

Sotuknang was right: the choice is ours. We have been given a beautiful Mother with whom we can live in perfect harmony. We have all that we need in this complete world prepared for us by our common Creator. Sustainability does not begin in the cold mathematics of production and consumption but rather in the human heart, in how we see the earth as a living being and how we choose to respect her in our exchange of mutual sharing.

Our decisions about how we understand and respond to the earth are apocalyptic. They are choices between life and death. They will determine how long this Fourth World will exist. Smohalla and the Dreamer religion recognized this reality and sought to defend the earth. They paid a heavy price, an apocalyptic price, for doing so. Their land was "claimed" in a different way, by a different philosophy, and it devastated their communities. The opposite of a living earth is a dying earth, and that specter of death hangs over our planet to this day.

— • —

In the Hopi chronicle of this Fourth World, the personification of death plays an important role. When humanity emerged into this world and began their search again for their place of wisdom and balance, they encountered the spirit who had been placed on the Earth to be its guardian and protector. This was Masauwu, one of the strangest figures in any religious tradition.

Masauwu was a hideous apparition. His face was disfigured as if he had been badly burned. His body was splattered by blood. His mouth was a gaping hole, and his eyes bulged from their sockets. His clothing was tattered and his hair matted. He was a spirit being who could not die like mortals, but who must have suffered grievous injury. According to Hopi tradition, he had once been a powerful spirit, but that power had gone to his head and he had lost his humility. He had brought down a disaster of his own making on himself and was left broken and helpless. He became the embodiment of death.

He would have remained in the underground of past worlds, except for the intervention of Tawa. The Creator desired reconciliation with Masauwu and appointed him to a new role as caretaker of the Earth. In the subtle genius of Hopi thought, death became the caretaker of life.

It is at this point that the Hopi narrative takes another turn into the mystical, for the story says that when the people met with Masauwu after their emergence into the Fourth World, they were sent out once again on their separate journeys. Their goal was to travel the earth, spiritually as well as physically, until they could return to find Masauwu one day at the right place, the center of creation. Among these people were those originally made from the four colors of clay: red, black, yellow, and white. The white clay people were called the Bahanas. Masauwu sent them on their way to the south, but after they had gone, some of the Hopi ancestors had an inspiration.

Masauwu had given the Fire Clan, one of the many clans of the Hopi people, a sacred tablet, etched with symbols to remind them of their sacred task. That tablet is said to still exist in the safekeeping of the clan, but it is broken. A piece is missing. That piece was deliberately broken by the Hopi and given to the Bahanas to carry with them. Masauwu told the Hopi that one day in the distant future, a time would come when they would be overcome by a strange people who had forgotten how to ask spiritual questions. These people without a memory would be descendants of the Bahanas. They would demand that the Hopi think like them or they would be punished.

The purpose of the broken tablet that Masauwu gave them was to provide the same chance for reconciliation that he had been given by Tawa. Among the Bahanas would be one person of good conscience, whose mind was still an open door to wisdom. That person would have the broken piece of the sacred tablet. When the two pieces were united, when the Hopi and the Bahanas were reconciled, then the Fourth World would be safe from the apocalypse. Centuries later, when the first conquistadores rode into Hopi villages, they were welcomed by the people as the long-lost clan of the Bahanas, a piece of the missing puzzle of a complete humanity. The Hopi extended the sacred tablet and waited for the Spanish to offer its broken fragment in return.

They are still waiting.

— • —

Wovoka, the prophet of the Ghost Dance, was waiting too. The echo of Hopi teaching in Wovoka's Ghost Dance is the echo of reconciliation. In all the controversy over the Ghost Dance, from the end of the nineteenth century and up to the present day, the question has remained: Did Wovoka see white people in his vision? Was his apocalyptic vision of a renewed earth for Native people only, or were the Americans to be included? After all the pain and suffering endured by the Indigenous people at the hand of the Bahanas, was reconciliation even possible?

The great tragedy of Wounded Knee shows us what happens when mutual respect and understanding are absent. It looks like Masauwu. It looks like death. The purpose of the Ghost Dance was reconciliation and restoration. It was an attempt to bring people back together. Like the Hopi tradition, part of that healing was bringing the clans of Indigenous people together, just as prophets like Tenskwatawa hoped. But it was also a challenge to racism and bigotry. Were the white people to be eradicated in the rebirth of the planet, or were they to be changed, forgiven, and reconciled?

Reconciliation is not pretty. It is often covered in blood. It demands a clear memory of what really happened, and that memory can be very ugly. So much of America's hope to be seen as a great nation remains buried beneath the snow of Wounded Knee. To resurrect it from the grave is like putting life in the hands of death. It is a fearful choice for both the Indigenous people of North America and their oppressors. It means facing one another in the clear light of history. It means acknowledging the truth. It means having the humility to ask for forgiveness in order to create a new future. Very often, when faced with that level of change, people from both clans, the oppressed and the oppressor, draw back and remain fixed in a position of anger and blame. Native people can keep wearing their ghost shirts. White people can keep denying anything really happened. But neither strategy works, and both leave us with a broken tablet of our own history.

The impact of boarding schools is a good example. Hopi children, like children from many Native American nations, were forcibly removed from their families, often at a very early age, and made to live in re-education centers called boarding schools. These institutions were often operated by churches and maintained the veneer that what they were doing was for the good of the children. In reality, they were brutal attempts to strip Indigenous identity, language, and culture from the children, to indoctrinate them into white values and norms. The children suffered physical, mental, and sexual abuse. More died than have been accounted for, their graves left unmarked.

This horrific part of North American history has long remained hidden. Now, as it is being slowly revealed, it provokes enormous sorrow and anger in the Indigenous community, and deep reactions of either guilt or denial from the white community. In graphic language, it is gut wrenching. Most people from both communities would not wish to long dwell on the scarring memories it raises.

But like Masauwu, we have to look at those scars. We have to not lose our memory, no matter how painful that memory may be. Life must reconcile with death. It was the Hopis' intention when they shared a piece of the sacred puzzle with their white relatives. It was the intention behind the Ghost Dance, when Indigenous people began dancing not only for themselves but for the whole of creation, including the Bahanas.

This world is called the Fourth World, sometimes known as the complete world, but it is not complete. Great pieces of the puzzle are still missing. The work of reconciliation is far from being accomplished. In the meantime, racism and bigotry are alive and well around us. They allow death to dominate life and leave us estranged and vulnerable to chaos. They invite another apocalypse to happen. They aid and abet the destruction that blights both communities through a willful closing of the mind and heart. Masauwu, who by his scars bears our stigmata, waits to see if we will all return to the center of the world, and by so doing, reconcile with one another as clans of the same family, equal in the eyes of Tawa, dancing together in a circle unbroken.

7

PROPHETS

We Are the Axis Point of the Apocalypse

The aggressive attitude that insists Native theories of religion are an insufficient basis for genuine comparative study has a long and painful history as a mirror image of the rhetoric of conquest which denied the spiritual values of Indian people. However, Native spiritual traditions have not been conquered, and they are more than mere survivors; they are resurgent, vital, and fully engaged in creative processes of social, communal, and cultural affirmation.

—Lee Irwin

HOW MANY TIMES have you survived the end of the world? If you are like most people, the answer is quite a few. And not just the big-ticket apocalypses of social unrest, natural disaster, or pandemic, but the personal apocalypse of loss, betrayal, or a broken heart. In fact, the large-scale collapse of routine can trigger the private apocalypse of any individual caught in the currents of cataclysm. When my ancestors walked the Trail of Tears in the 1830s, refugees driven from their homes and death-marched to a strange new land, they suffered not only as a community but as individuals. They lost homes, family, even gravesites that were precious to them.

Apocalypse is more than just an image of the end of the world, although it has come to symbolize that in the popular imagination. There can be more than one apocalypse in a lifetime. In fact, as human beings, we may struggle through several apocalyptic experiences and spend a great deal of time striving to make sense of them. Whether it is a global meltdown or a personal crisis: the impact of these events are deep and lasting.

We live in an atmosphere of apocalypse. Remember that apocalypse is two things: an actual event and a revelation. Together, these two aspects combine into what we call the apocalyptic process. It is, to borrow a phrase from the Bible, both wars and rumors of wars. Prophets arise within the context of this process. They announce the impending arrival of an apocalypse or they seek to help their communities cope with one that is already happening. Therefore, prophets become entry points into the nature of any apocalypse. They show us strategies to cope with what we are afraid we cannot control.

In our contemporary situation, this approach is important because so many of us are feeling caught in the apocalyptic process. We are hearing more disturbing news about our future, while at the same time, we are trying to manage the crises already at hand. We are an anxious generation. We want a new way to both understand apocalypse and navigate our way through it.

In making this exploration into the meaning and management of apocalypse, both as event and as revelation, we have turned to the Native American experience of North America. We know that Indigenous communities have not only confronted enormous apocalyptic histories but have come through that trauma with their cultures still alive and growing. We want to know more about what these Native nations can teach us all about living through an apocalypse. Therefore, we have listened to the story of four Native American prophets and considered what their messages have to teach us. To deepen our understanding, we have placed those four prophets into an even larger apocalyptic narrative, the creation saga of the Hopi people. In this way we have looked back to see how the American Apocalypse—in essence, the colonial history of North America—was endured by Native nations and how their spiritual resilience allowed them to survive.

Now we need to look ahead. As our study of apocalypse becomes a revelation, what does it show us about our future?

It is at this point that I have to take the risk of being a prophet. It is a role I believe any of us can take on. In this broad view, the role of the prophet is not dependent on any special knowledge or magical abilities. It does not imply some special level of righteousness or purity. As we have already seen, prophets can be people with problems. Two of the prophets in this book were severely alcoholic. All four were accused of being fraudulent and manipulative. From what we know of their individual histories, none were necessarily easy persons to be around. When I was a little boy, I heard my elders say, "Clean water can still come through a broken pipe." A perfect message does not have to be relayed by a perfect messenger. We can all stand to offer our wisdom. We are worthy of being heard.

Whether people accept the prophecy we lift up is another matter. None of our four Native prophets received universal appreciation, even among their own people. The old saying about a prophet not finding honor in her or his home community is a truism rarely debated. We can take the risk of sharing our own vision, but it is always a risk. A prophet may be ignored, scorned, or even silenced. There is no guarantee of acceptance, as many exiled or condemned prophets have already discovered.

I don't expect you will want to burn me at the stake for what I will say in this chapter, but you may find it challenging to embrace. I realize I am taking a gamble, but I am willing to do so because I think the apocalyptic stakes are so high. Therefore, my first prophetic act is to name the situation we confront before I offer the revelation of what we can do about it.

In doing this, let me be transparent that I am speaking from the context of Indigenous North American history and spirituality. I am not speaking for all Native people, but only for myself. However, I am speaking as a Native person who honors his ancestors by seeking to live a spiritual life in accordance with their traditions. That is why I have spent time looking into the prophets of our people and why knowing the foundational stories like those the Hopi relate are so important to me.

Like all Indigenous people, I am a survivor. I have faced the brutal reality of our history as a colonized people. I have not looked away from the truth of our suffering. I have also been intentional about coping with the personal trauma this kind of history creates. So many of my people were lost to an old apocalypse, so many more are being lost to its aftershocks in this generation. Suicide rates among my people are high. Alcoholism, drug dependency, depression, abusive behavior: the personal apocalypse in many lives continues. I did not learn to cope with either the historic apocalypse of my nation or the individual apocalypse still haunting my people on my own, but with the spiritual help of my elders. Their wisdom and teachings sustained me. Their courage and vision inspired me. For me, the Trail of Tears has ended. The path to wholeness, transformation, and reconciliation has begun. What I share in this chapter is what I have discerned so far, not only from the material in this book but from a lifetime of reflection on and engagement with the Native tradition that has formed me.

— • —

What do we see after every apocalypse we survive? What lessons do we learn, over and over again? As is so often the case in the conduct of human beings, there are positive answers and negative answers. On the negative side of the debriefing we often discover the root cause of the apocalypse is ourselves. Human greed, neglect, ambition, racism, indifference: our detective work after an apocalypse very often reveals that the core problem was in our own behavior. On the positive side of the ledger we may find the most effective response to the apocalypse was also ourselves. Human courage, kindness, cooperation, compassion, common sense: we discover, once again, the best of ourselves when the reality of the apocalypse is at its worst.

Essentially, what we learn is that we, human beings, are the axis point for apocalypse. While there are many natural disasters to which we must respond and over which we have no control—earthquakes, for example, or volcanic eruptions—there are many more initiated by human actions. Wars and political oppression are two primary examples. In individual lives and local communities there are a host of smaller but very damaging apocalyptic events that impact us all: racial prejudice, religious intolerance, misogyny, rejection of other human beings based on sexual orientation. While we cannot stop a tsunami or volcano, we can stop a great many, if not all, forms of apocalypse.

Our apocalyptic irony is that we suffer while the solution is right before us. When I was a young activist opposing the war in Vietnam, one poster became a ubiquitous part of that era. It simply said, *What if they gave a war and nobody came?* As simplistic as that sentiment may seem, it contains a deep truth. It is by people's choice to participate that tyrannies rise and fall. If more people joined the effort to halt environmental decline while fewer people actively aided and abetted it, what would happen? If political parties that supported oppression lost members while political groups supporting justice grew in numbers, what would happen?

There is no great mystery to the apocalyptic process. We create much of it ourselves, and we can change much of it.

We can break the cycles of apocalypse we find ourselves in. We can alter the path of history: 90 percent of our success will be in just showing up.

We are the axis point of apocalypse. The degree to which we participate in the apocalyptic process can tip the scales and determine the outcome. Therefore, our greatest problem is not necessarily the event itself but our reaction to it. Resignation is the challenge. Over the centuries, prophets far wiser than me have pointed out the obvious: we have the power to generate apocalyptic disasters, and we have the power to control them. These prophetic voices have sought to shake people awake from sleepwalking into an apocalypse because they are in a state of resignation. Prophets have tried to inspire people to believe that we are not helpless but capable. When H. G. Wells wrote his science fiction classic *The Time Machine*, he projected a distant future, after a long cycle of apocalyptic suffering, where human beings become docile creatures of resignation, waiting to die while doing nothing.

Resignation dulls the mind. Like a narcotic it puts us into an ethical trance and leaves us immobilized in the face of danger. We watch wars come and go, dictators rise and fall, the poor struggle and die, imagining that this is the way it was meant to be, resigning ourselves to the role of spectators to our own demise rather than participants in our shared salvation.

Cruel observers from another planet might say we get what we deserve, but to me that judgment is unfair. There are mitigating circumstances for our action—or rather, our lack of action. As a human family we have lived with this instinct for resignation for millennia. It is baked into our cultures. It is imprinted on our psyche. We are primates who have suffered the domination of the alpha male and subconsciously imagine that we cannot break that spell. As our cultures grew ever more complex, they brought with them the reality we experienced on the ancient savannas where our most distant ancestors lived. At the center of human life is an instinct for resignation, a fear that makes us participate in our own oppression. It began when we lived in troops among the trees, and it continued when we set our first king on his throne of power.

Waking up from the hypnosis of resignation is the first step in transforming the apocalyptic process. The four prophets we have considered in these pages each began their mission in a state of resignation. They all "fell asleep" or "died" before their trip to the afterlife. Prior to that they had been resigned to the reality of their apocalypse, observers to the demise of all they loved.

But once they awakened they became agents of change. The spell of helplessness was broken. The weak became strong. The prophets embodied that strength. They showed people what was possible. In one way, the spiritual power of their message was not necessarily in what they *taught* but rather in what they *did*, what they demonstrated. The generic story of the prophet going into a trance, "dying to this world," and then miraculously coming back to life: that is the most fundamental hope they conveyed. All four of them were physically challenged. All four of them were powerless before their prophetic experience. All four were moving with their people on the conveyor belt of colonialism to their destruction. They physically demonstrated that fact when they fell to the ground, rigid and unmoving.

There was nothing they could do to save their people other than one thing: wake up.

— • —

In the widespread prophetic tradition of Native America, this act of awakening from a trance is the critical moment. The sleep state, resignation, is broken when the seer returns with her or his message. Let's consider this pivotal part of Indigenous prophecy carefully. The awakening is the axis point between resignation and action. The four prophets, along with countless others throughout Native American history, symbolized that spiritual hinge point for their communities. They showed us what has to happen before change can occur. We have to wake up. We have to see reality clearly and understand our part as participants in it. In the Native American spiritual context, we have to receive our vision.

What makes a person a prophet? We all share in the existential reality of the prophet; that is, we are human. We are limited, finite, fallible people who think we have very little power when it comes to confronting an apocalypse. Our resignation is not so much giving up as it is never imagining otherwise. We assume we are born into such a weak position in relation to the world that there is nothing we can do to alter it, not fundamentally, not historically. We may be able to do some small acts of grace in our immediate cultural neighborhood, but we do not imagine we have any authority beyond those narrow boundaries. More than this, many of us are conditioned by the dominant culture to have an even lower estimation of ourselves. Women, people of color, people of different sexual orientations: we can be intentionally marginalized, and sometimes we internalize our own oppression.

Waking up from this illusion is what Native American tradition calls the vision quest. Vision may come unbidden, as it did for our four prophets, but it can also come when we seek it for ourselves. The four prophets each received a vision in a sudden and unexpected way. In this sense they were chosen by a higher power for the role they played in their community. But Native American tradition does not limit the visionary experience to prophets alone. It is a spiritual awakening open to every person. Before Smohalla had his great vision of the afterlife, he had been on his own vision quest. As he trained to be a medicine person, Tenskwatawa would have certainly undertaken a vision quest, perhaps more than once. Ganiodaiio was intent on maintaining the ancient spiritual practices of his people, and one of those practices was the vision quest. So while we may not all become historic figures as prophets, we can all aspire to receive a vision if we choose to look for it.

Part of the egalitarian nature of traditional Native American cultures is this recognition that spiritual vision is accessible to all people, not only to a few. That is a critical thing for us to understand. If we are feeling powerless against the reality around us, the concept of a vision quest opens a door to us. It shows us how to tap into a deeper strength with a more focused response. The beginning of resignation is the idea that our perception of reality is flawed—for example, that we are not smart enough, important enough, or holy enough to understand the apocalypse, much less deal with it. The beginning of our spiritual self-confidence is that we have direct access to a power far beyond the limitations of our own perceptions. There is a higher power that wants us to participate, wants us to let go of resignation, and will show us how.

Ganiodaiio helped his people cope with the apocalypse of their time by giving them a sense of self-worth.

He reversed the polarity of his culture to put the focus on the individual. He breathed new life into the Great Law of Peace that had been the core of their belief system by helping each person believe they were a valuable part of it. To create community, he first had to create individuals: people who were proud of themselves and had a shared confidence in their future. The individual vision of each man and woman was acknowledged and honored. They all became stakeholders in their combined future.

In our context, that same kind of "cultural adjustment" is going to be necessary, only in reverse. As a scattered collection of individuals, raised to think we are powerless, we are going to need a new vision of ourselves as people capable of change. Waking up to our power is waking up to community.

How do we learn to trust one another? How do we work together for the common good? How do we communicate without the filter of fear and suspicion? Our vision quest is a search for answers to those questions. We are on a search for a new corporate vision. We are looking for something we can all believe in together. Like the Great Law of Peace, it may be something we have known for a long while but that needs to be renewed and extended. We each have our individual vision, but we must find a way to embody those visions in a collective way, especially in times of conflict or danger.

We need Tenskwatawa's city on the hill. We need a Prophetstown.

— • —

The change from individualism to individuality, the finding of unity in diversity, is the vision we seek. In searching for community we often point to moments when great disasters or conflicts threw people together. London during the Blitz, the German bombing campaign of 1940 and 1941, is an example of this phenomenon, as is the communal spirit that arose during the Great Depression. And while these examples are true, they are also limited. Yes, community can be discovered in the bomb shelter, but will it last once the all-clear has been sounded and we step outside again? Does our unity continue after the apocalypse—or is it only the product of intense pressure?

Tenskwatawa and his brother Tecumseh did their best to build a community based on a threat from the outside. They failed. Not that the community at Prophetstown was not genuine; it was, for as long as it lasted. The Native people who came to the village were filled with hope. They put aside their many differences to unite into a new understanding of Native identity and nationhood. And yet if Tenskwatawa's experience teaches us anything, it's that fear alone cannot transform us from our past divisions.

An apocalypse may very well bring us together to meet an imminent danger, but once that apocalypse has receded, it will not be strong enough to keep us together. Something greater than fear is needed to build community. Part of our vision quest must be to find that something so we can become the beacon for which we are searching.

The Hopi give us a clue. The record of their long migrations, carved into the desert around them, reveals a vision of community grounded in a different and more permanent soil than outside pressure. Hopi community arises from a vision of human beings as fellow travelers on a journey of discovery. In Hopi spirituality we are always on the verge of a new migration. We are propelled by our inner nature as people who must ask questions. Our job it is to carry the collective memory of humanity into the future.

Hopi prophecy can sound like science fiction to us because it is so far advanced of its historical location. As we have seen, the Hopi had a concept of spiritual physics when their European counterparts were just emerging from a flat earth mindset. The Hopi worldview embraced a vision of the earth as an integrated system for navigating through time. They understood that over time, long spans of time, the land could change, plants and animals could change, people could change—but the one constant was the ark of humanity, a diverse community, chosen by the Creator for a special mission.

Our future, the Hopi would say, is in the next Emergence. Our role is to find that new opening. We must discover new ways to continue an ancient story. We are all on a vision quest together. We are searching for the path through apocalypse to a new beginning. That quest is not complete without every piece of the puzzle. We need the combined intellect and experience of all people to safely guide our journey into its next emergence. As limited as we may be individually, our future will be secured if we remember we are all clans of the same migration. This is not a trip for the Hopi alone, but for all of us who believe our task is to transform apocalypse into hope.

The community this kind of thinking produced among the Hopi is one of the most enduring on the planet. While the American Apocalypse descended on the Hopi, with all its shock-and-awe tactics for conquest, it failed to overwhelm Hopi tradition. Hopi spiritual resilience was stronger than an apocalypse. I believe this is because Hopi tradition is not completely grounded in the here and now. The vision on the hill of a new community has been tried before in many different ways. Each of those ways has eventually succumbed to the contemporary pressures of history. The utopian dreams that people like Marx and Engels sought, the perfect theocracies envisioned by the Puritans: all these failed to be sustainable. They were eclipsed by change in the world that surrounded them. But the Hopi concept of community has survived for thousands of years, perhaps for longer than we will ever know. Like the Aboriginal people of Australia, they have an ancient concept of life that is dream-like in its vision. What they see is not just a city on a hill in our historical reality, but a community in the stars, a future civilization inhabiting new worlds as part of a story that never ends.

The Hopi create community, not out of fear but out of dreams. Human aspiration, human imagination, is the cornerstone of their invitation to us. Tenskwatawa was right: we need a clear and inviting focal point to draw humanity together. But that focal point must be greater than our own apocalypse of the moment. We cannot stay in the bomb shelter together forever. At some point we are going to need to emerge into the clear light of day. What will hold us together then? If we are spiritual explorers who need one another for the perilous journey to come, then we need a transcendent vision of life to hold us together, a commitment to life that is unequivocal.

— • —

Smohalla showed us that commitment. The unique thing about the kind of community we hope to create for all people is that it is not just for human beings but for all life. The earth that we guide into the next emergence is as alive as we are. It breathes. It grows. It dies. As Smohalla taught, it also thinks and feels. The community we seek in our vision quest is a relationship, an intimate relationship. If the Hopi give us a more scientific way to envision that relationship, the Dreamers give us a vocabulary to describe it that is intentionally emotional. Prophets like Smohalla and leaders like Chief Joseph speak in a way about Mother Earth that leaves no doubt about their spiritual perspective: the earth is not inanimate. It is alive. If we are spiritually awake, we recognize this fact and we understand that we are living in a covenant, an agreement, with this living world. Other covenant-based religions may describe community as a willingness to obey the letter of the law in that agreement, but for Native American prophets, community requires each person to embrace the vision of the earth as a living being. Covenant is not law. It is love.

When the Dreamer vision speaks of the earth in intimate terms, we need to take that literally. Native tradition does recognize the imagery used by prophets like Smohalla as factual references to our relationship with the planet. Indigenous theology is saying a personal relationship with the earth is real. This is exactly what the Dreamers said to the generals who were trying to drive them off their land. The relationship to Mother Earth is both conscious and reciprocal. Native American tradition recognizes the real presence of life incarnate in the planet. This may be a great mystery to human beings, but it is nonetheless an accurate depiction of sacred reality.

We do not control the earth, for she has a mind of her own. We do not own the earth, for she can live without us while we cannot live without her. We do not abuse the earth, for her life can be as fragile as ours. Instead, we live in relationship with her. At times, this can be an apocalyptic relationship. The natural life of our planet can bring great storms, earthquakes, and volcanoes. But it can also bring us what we need to sustain ourselves: rainfall, fertile soil, plants, and animals in both variety and abundance. Our covenant is a symbiotic loving relationship.

Love is the key word. For many years now scientists have been prophets of our covenant relationship with the earth. They have tried to warn us that we are impacting the earth so negatively that life itself is hanging in the balance. This threat seems adequate to compel us to cooperate for short periods of time, but it has not been sufficient to bond us into concerted action with enough determination to alter our course, even though we can clearly see where neglect is taking us. If scientific facts are not able to sway us, and fear of the future is not great enough to get us to change, then perhaps the call of the Dreamers can be a tipping point.

As most of the world's religions will attest, love is one of the most powerful forces on earth. Love endures whether there is external pressure or not. Love can bring strangers together and it can hold them together through all seasons of life. Love has authority in our lives just as it has enormous healing capacity. Therefore, love is valuable to us. Our combined experience as human beings over centuries has shown us that love has value. The vision we seek is the revelation of love's value over and beyond the value we give to material possessions.

The struggle we face is the same struggle of the Native American prophets: to help people wake up—in this case, to wake up to the understanding that our environmental apocalypse is an issue of the heart. Unless we love the earth, just as we would love another human being, our future is grim. And while this may seem simplistic to some cultures, for Native American tradition it has been fundamental. The experience of Indigenous people demonstrates that it is possible to build a civilization based on respect for the earth rather than her exploitation. Destroying the earth for the sake of profit is predicated on the value of more. Love is predicated on the value of enough to share. The wealth obsession that has dominated some cultures in history is not a reality set in stone. It is not normative. Native communities have existed for centuries in a balanced relationship with the earth that spoke of having enough to share, not the accumulation of more for the few over the many.

Tenskwatawa sought that certain place, the sacred place to create community. What I am saying is that the earth herself is that certain place. The community we need to develop is a community of not just human beings but of life with the Mother and all her relations. The apocalyptic reality we confront in our lifetime is a radical change in the priorities of our global community.

The history of colonialism is the story of domination by those who benefit from a dead-earth vision of more for the few. For a very long time now, we have been seduced into believing that only the exploitation model is real. The Indigenous opinion—we have enough that we can share— has been denigrated as primitive, simplistic, or naive. Real civilizations are cultures of accumulation. They march forward over the back of the earth, taking what they need to bring more wealth to those in positions of power. We have been trained to admire that kind of rugged individualism. We have been recruited into a spiritual Ponzi scheme that hides the fact that this worldview is not sustainable.

Who is naive here: the culture that still believes the earth cannot die, or the culture that believes she is as real as you or me?

— • —

The Hopi tradition, along with that of all Indigenous people, is living proof that human beings can live in a loving relationship with the earth. The benefits of that balanced relationship are clear. The earth can provide enough for all to share. Environmental apocalypse can be averted. A healthier planet can be achieved if we have the will to work together as people with a common Mother. Although it has been eclipsed and devalued, the Indigenous alternative is still here, still existing beneath the shadow of colonialism. Greed has not yet won the day. There is still time if we act now and if we act as one family.

But how do we become that family? That is the question, because the forces of exploitation have left us shattered and suspicious. We are divided by racism and classism. We are pitted against one another as the chasm between the haves and have-nots grows wider. The politics of fear drives us into the bunkers of our opinions, trading the truth of our shared reality for the imaginary safety of our isolation. Given the depth of that social oppression, what can we do to overcome it?

We can start dancing.

Wovoka raised the apocalyptic question of the afterlife: Who is going to get to go to heaven? In other words, in his vision of a restored Mother, a world of enough to share for everyone, who would the "everyones" be? Would it just be some of us, a few of us, or all of us? Was it reserved for Native people alone or would the white people be there as well? The debate over Wovoka's vision was a turning point in Native American history and it was part of a much larger history than even the Prophet himself may have known.

Over the centuries religions have answered the question of who gets to go to heaven in a wide variety of ways. Very often the answer has been exclusionary. Only the followers of this faith or that faith will make it. All the others will perish. The apocalypse in the last book of the Bible is a powerful example of this kind of gatekeeper faith. It emerges from a history of apocalypse where survival was uncertain. The persecution of early Christians drove the religion underground, just as the persecution of the Ghost Dance drove Native believers underground. The difference, however, is that Christian theology responded by becoming more exclusive, while Indigenous theology became more inclusive.

According to his original vision, Wovoka saw white people and people of all other races in the postapocalyptic world. In other words, he saw a future reconciliation with the settlers. Given the history between the two cultures, this vision is as startling as if the author of the book of Revelation had pictured the Christian martyrs enjoying the afterlife with the people who threw them to the lions.

It is a huge step toward reconciliation and, like the book of Revelation, it has a long history behind it. Wovoka's vision emerges from the spiritual tradition among Indigenous people that goes back to the Hopi prophecy of the lost tablet. The theological assumption behind both Wovoka and the Hopi is that human beings are created equal and that we need one another to be whole. The missing piece of the puzzle for Native America is reconciliation with the very people who stole their land and tried to exterminate them. By any stretch of the spiritual imagination, that is an astonishing thing to do.

Reconciliation is not for the fainthearted. In fact, it is such a daunting assignment that very few may believe it is actually possible. And yet, it is only one of many other historical apocalypses that have torn people apart, all of which need reconciliation. As the human family, how many genocides have we endured? How may wholesale pogroms and persecutions? How many wars of extermination? The story of human cruelty and hatred runs deep in many histories. Racism has fueled the pain of slavery until it is burned into our memory. Religious wars have slaughtered millions of people in the name of God. The greed of exploitation has forced many cultures to the brink of annihilation. To imagine a reconciliation capable of redeeming such a history seems impossible. Which explains why people on both sides of the American Apocalypse saw Wovoka's vision in the only way they could believe credible. Many Native people saw it as a means to carry on the fight, while many white people saw it as another excuse for genocide.

The Spanish conquistadores looked at the Hopi with derision when they were welcomed as the long lost siblings of an ancient story. They could not comprehend a worldview that would make them equal to the people they wanted to conquer. And yet according to the Hopi vision, the apocalypse of our suffering will not stop until we are all reunited as one family. The plan of creation will not be complete until we finally overcome the spiritual blindness of racism, misogyny, religious intolerance, and moral scapegoating. As impossible as it seems, our task is to become Ghost Dancers because we share in Wovoka's vision: we believe reconciliation is possible. No matter how incredible, no matter how painful, we believe it can happen.

The key is in the dance. The strange dance with no music.

Ghost Dancers dance in silence. The only sound is the movement of their feet and the chant they share as an appeal to heaven. In other words, the dancers have to make their own music. The rhythm comes from within. In the silence we are the same. Imagine a circle of human beings, brought together from different cultures, silent except for one song they can sing together. No arguments, no denials, no justifications. No politics, no religion, no philosophy. Only what they can sing together, the same song that their hearts already know.

This ancient song is the one the Hopi understood as the one we shared before human beings separated to follow their own paths of migration around the world. The original language of human hope: the need for food, for shelter, for love. These ancient needs are the same in every culture. They are the memory of what we first valued. Family, children, safety, death in the company of those we love. The Hopi are memory bearers for humanity. They tell us what our ancestors—all of our ancestors, not just a select few—once understood. In carrying out the Ghost Dance we are reconnecting with those ancestors, the "ghosts" of our common past, gone but not forgotten.

— • —

Reconciliation begins in recollection. Like time travelers, we must remember earlier worlds. We have to move silently back through the years, the blood-soaked years of our past, the truth of what we have done to one another, until we leave behind all of our agendas except for one thing: our common humanity. It is not as difficult as you might think. That silent circle of people from different migrations can begin to sing together when they speak of their primal values: their children and their grandchildren. Love of family is a song we all know by heart. There are others. So many ways to connect to an older memory, before the days of our separation.

As deep as the divide between us may be, with horrific images of past atrocities, the bridge over this pain is right before us: our memory of the beginning. Wovoka's prophecy asks us to gather the dancers from every community, all those willing to take the risk, and let them enter the circle in silence, aware only of one another's presence in the dance. Hands joined, moving together in silence, until the sound of the human heart sings the memory of our ancestors, the time when we were still the same.

Intentional efforts to heal the scars of racism, including truth and reconciliation events, involve the recitation of past abuses. They force us to remember our painful and ugly past. It is a cathartic experience. I have been in gatherings of Indigenous people and the descendants of white settlers. I have sat in rooms where the truth of the horrors of boarding schools have been recounted by those who survived them. The stories of the physical, emotional, and sexual abuse of Native children have left me in tears of sorrow and anger. The stories are difficult to hear, but they are absolutely necessary if people want to understand how far apart history has taken us. And if that recitation of pain was all I experienced, then I think I would have left without much hope for the future. Genuine reconciliation would seem impossible.

But the truth telling itself was not the whole story. Like most every gathering of human beings, there were breaks for lunch and dinner. Looking out over a group of people eating together at one of these events, I had a revelation. I finally understood the Hopi prophecy.

The same people who had just been together in a profoundly painful exchange of memory were now sitting at tables together breaking bread with one another. How mundane a moment at such a serious gathering: the basic human need to eat. How perfectly natural to share the food together. How completely human for people to make small talk over a meal. Stories of their children. Stories to make others laugh. Stories of trips to foreign lands. It was all right there before me. The Hopi prophecy that we are all alike.

Beneath all the layers of misery and triumph, the simple but eternal realities that make us who we are, the tribe of the human beings. As harsh as our history may be, the irrepressible sameness of our core being is always there, just beneath the surface. It is ancient and it is accessible. It is Wovoka's silent vision of people doing what people like to do: the quiet need of any person seeking to share a common fire on a cold night.

Reconciliation is possible and, as the prophets have shown us, absolutely necessary if we are to withstand the next wave of an apocalypse. In fact, reconciliation will help to mitigate, if not prevent, another apocalypse of social upheaval, environmental disaster, and racial injustice. For too long our human family has been victimized by a spiritual amnesia. We have forgotten what the Hopi tell us we must remember: the time and place of our origin. The simple realities of our common life are mnemonics for our ancient memory of a time when we were all part of the clans of a single community. They take us back to the vision of unity that has eluded us for centuries. They remind us that race, language, and culture are only colors of clay—the same clay from which we were all fashioned. As horrific as our history may be, the truth is written on the rocks. We were once all the same. We can be again. Reconciliation is a return. It is an act of regaining our memory. What Wovoka saw was both past and future, the coming full circle of the long migration of humanity. We can heal from our forgetfulness and become what we must become to meet the next world that is already before us.

What the four prophets and the Hopi teach us is a way to engage apocalypse as revelation. They show us that we must have a vision of ourselves that replaces rugged individualism with creative individuality. We must be committed to a community that transcends our own history by breaking down the walls that have kept us apart. To do that, we need a shared vision, an ideal to which we can all offer our allegiance. By definition, that certain place must embody diversity. It must be grounded in a recognition of the earth as a living part of an ancient covenant. We must reject the idea of more for the few and proclaim enough for the many. And to make all of this happen, we need to rediscover our memory as an act of deep reconciliation throughout the human family. As painful as it may be to tell the truth, we will find that pain far more bearable than the lie of our imagined difference. Only in this way can our migration from apocalypse to wholeness continue. Only together in harmony with creation can we find our way home.

EPILOGUE

YOU ARE A
PROPHET BECAUSE
YOU ARE AWAKE

IN MY OPENING chapter I said that hope would have
the last word in this book. While it is a book that talks
about historical realities and the visionary prophets who
responded to them, it is fundamentally a book about you
and me and all of us together who confront an apocalypse.
It is for everyone who thinks it is time to wake up.

Do you feel you are living on the threshold of an apocalypse? Do you get the sense that things are collapsing
around you? Do you ever wish you had an escape plan to
get away from reality before it comes crashing down? If
you do, then please do not think I am being flippant when
I say welcome to the human family. A great many of us
feel that way today, and a great many of our ancestors felt

that way over the past millennia. Like us, they faced the apocalypses of their time and they survived.

But how? That is the question. Do we simply endure moments of apocalyptic change, trying to survive as best we can? Or do we engage the apocalypse, using our insight to navigate it or perhaps even avoid it altogether?

In this book we have made the proactive choice. We have listened to wisdom from a part of the human family that has weathered the end of the world many times and lived to tell about it. Native American nations have endured war, genocide, pandemics, concentration camps, re-education centers, death marches, religious persecution, environmental disaster, language loss, imprisonment, political oppression, sanctioned murder, kidnapping, slavery, sexual abuse, and endemic racism. And yet, sovereign Native nations are still here. They have not only survived; they have grown stronger.

And the remarkable thing about this remarkable story is that Native people did so not as superbeings, but as everyday people. What they discovered, we can all discover. What they learned, we can all learn. Explaining its resilience does not require that the history of Native America be clothed in mysticism, like Rousseau's noble savage, or manipulated to fit an agenda, like Marx's perfect utopia. The endurance of Native America comes from sources within every culture. It is the hope of all humanity.

What the four prophets and the Hopi reveal to us are abilities within us all to not only get through an apocalypse but to actively reshape its impact and trajectory. The Native experience offers us the tools we need to build a future rather than suffer a future. These are not exotic artifacts of a people from the distant past. What Native prophecy shows us are not New Age mysteries of spirit animals or private visions of an exotic shaman. The tools of Native America are spiritually pragmatic options based on centuries of human experience. They are as old as the Hopi migrations. They are practical insights that can be replicated by any people of any time.

Ganiodaiio showed us that each of us is responsible for what is happening around us. We are a part of it. We cannot avoid or evade responsibility. We must confess this truth, not by an endless recitation of our own complicity but by concrete actions that respond to the needs of others. We must think in the "we," not the "me." Cultures built on entitlement, privilege, and oligarchy will not survive, but collapse under the apocalyptic pressure of injustice and corruption. Egalitarian communities have a chance of making the changes they need to adapt and to evolve.

Tenskwatawa showed us the need for a fixed place on which to make our stand. This is not the shifting sands of endless competition for power and wealth, but a solid foundation on which we can build together. Diversity is that sacred ground. Inclusivity and respect are the framework for our place of welcome for the stranger. Unity is the key to overcoming an apocalypse, and unity depends on the ability to see in others what we most value in ourselves. Together we build the city on the hill we have all been seeking.

Smohalla showed us that the core of our survival is not technological or utilitarian but relational. We can extract all that the earth has to give until the last person standing is monarch of a wasteland. Or we can acknowledge the living presence of the earth as our Mother and create a truly sustainable future. Our attitude alone may be the hinge point of apocalypse. What we see in nature is what we get.

Wovoka showed us a glimpse of what must be accomplished if we are to weather an apocalypse and have something of value to bequeath to our children. Truth and reconciliation is the process we must engage, no matter how painful it may be. Racism will not end without an intervention, and only when we deal with the ghosts of our past will we see our whole family living at peace in a life abundant with hope. Our vision must be broad enough to include those with whom we have always struggled. No one goes to the promised land unless we all go together.

The Hopi showed us that all of the above is part of an ancient and mysterious story. We are all from the same place or origin. We are all going to the same place of a shared destiny. The human migration has begun and will not end until we have made our final pilgrimage. Whether that is into a final apocalypse or a journey to the stars depends on the choices we make. We travel through a sacred space of questions. We travel with an open mind and an open heart. We find life in the midst of death.

— • —

If these prophetic messages have touched your spirit—if they have awakened in you a renewed energy to engage the apocalypse—then I invite you to join me in becoming a prophet. I invite you to take what you have learned in this book and put it to use. It does not matter what your race or religion may be. It does not matter what age or gender you are. We can all become prophets of our own time. We are all needed. Apocalyptic times give rise to apocalyptic visions, and the bearers of those visions are the everyday people who are willing to take the risk of sharing them.

We are all prophets. We are not divine messengers. We do not speak for God. We are not miracle workers or moral judges. Instead, we are what the four prophets were: human beings living in extraordinary times. We are what the Hopi are: communities seeking a spiritual purpose to their lives. We are question askers. We are vision seekers.

We strive to be common-sense advocates for what will work best to help our people.

There is a sense of urgency about what I am inviting you to be. I am asking you to intentionally assume the role of a prophet to underscore that urgency. The life of a prophet is not easy. Urging others to confront reality, work together, and make sacrifices for the sake of change is never popular. Sharing authority in community, welcoming the stranger, negotiating differences is always a challenge. But we must do all these things and more if we are to transform the apocalypse of our time.

The moment of emergence is drawing near. Already we have crossed many thresholds in our relationship to Mother Earth that cannot be altered. The divisions between us are deep and growing deeper. The signs of our history are etched on the rocks for all to see. I do not say these things to rattle the old bones of fear and doom but to awaken us to the role we have been offered. We do not have to enter a trance to see our vision. We are already Dreamers. We are already in the circle of the Ghost Dance. Prophetstown is where we are in the here and now.

So I hope you will share the message in this book with as many as you can. I hope you will see it as a personal invitation to join me, and millions of others, in the prophetic work of coping with apocalypse. I hope you will use it as a source of support in the hard work of change. Believe in yourself. You are a prophet. You are already making your migration. You have been chosen because you have been born. You are a prophet because you are awake. You are a keeper of revelation: a person with a thought that may create a new world. Do not hide that piece of the sacred tablet, for the time is short, but give it to as many as you can, as often as you can, until the apocalypse becomes a blessing.

NOTES

CHAPTER 2

Hadawa'ko—also known by the honorific name Ganio-daiio: Most traditional Native Americans have more than one name in a lifetime. To avoid confusion and to honor Indigenous languages, I will refer to the four prophets by their traditional titles or names.

The clan mothers had a pivotal role: Alfred A. Cave, *Prophets of the Great Spirit* (Lincoln: University of Nebraska Press, 2006), 216.

American armies in 1779 systematically burned villages: Cave, *Prophets of the Great Spirit*, 184.

Felt the love of God flowing powerfully: Anthony F. C. Wallace, *The Death and Rebirth of the Seneca* (New York: Vintage Books, 1972), 242.

The Great Spirit has appointed four Angels: Wallace, *Death and Rebirth of the Seneca*, 267.

The day was bright: Wallace, *Death and Rebirth of the Seneca*, 318.

I will soon go to my new home: Wallace, *Death and Rebirth of the Seneca*, 320.

Handsome Lake kept alive many: Cave, *Prophets of the Great Spirit*, 223–24.

It is, therefore, no surprise: See Engels's treatise, *The Origin of the Family, Private Property and the State*, in *Karl Marx & Frederick Engels: Selected Works* (New York: International Publishers, 1977), 518–30.

Handsome Lake, responding to cultural and economic stress: Alf H. Walle, *The Path of Handsome Lake: A Model of Recovery for Native People* (Greenwich, CT: Information Age Publishing, 2004), 112.

His Gaiwiio set in motion: Wallace, *Death and Rebirth of the Seneca*, 303.

CHAPTER 3

We wish to draw the Indians to agriculture: Peter Cozzens, *Tecumseh and the Prophet* (New York: Vintage Books, 2020), 144.

A year later, in 1804: Cozzens, *Tecumseh and the Prophet*, 145.

To add to the intimidation: R. David Edmunds, *The Shawnee Prophet* (Lincoln: University of Nebraska Press, 1985), 23.

These missionaries "baptized" converts: Cozzens, *Tecumseh and the Prophet*, 163.

If he is really a prophet: Edmunds, *The Shawnee Prophet*, 47.

Just at the darkest moment of the eclipse: Edmunds, *The Shawnee Prophet*, 49.

This was the great council house: Cozzens, *Tecumseh and the Prophet*, 158.

Reflected their ignorance about the nature of his influence: Edmunds, *The Shawnee Prophet*, 62–63.

What did he name the little spot: Cozzens, *Tecumseh and the Prophet*, 432.

CHAPTER 4

My father sent for me: Bob Blaisdell, *Great Speeches by Native Americans* (Mineola, NY: Dover Publications, 2000), 149.

Tell General Howard I know his heart: Blaisdell, *Great Speeches by Native Americans,* 148.

A holy covenant existed between God and man: Clifford E. Trafzer and Margery Ann Beach, "Smohalla, the Washani, and Religion as a Factor in Northwest Indian History," *The American Indian Quarterly* 9, no. 3 (1985): 311.

Nothing resulting from the American presence: Robert H. Ruby and John A. Brown, *Dreamer-Prophets of the Columbia Plateau* (Norman: University of Oklahoma Press, 1989), 11.

We simply take the gifts that are freely offered: Ruby and Brown, *Dreamer-Prophets of the Columbia Plateau,* 33.

You asked me to plough the ground: Ruby and Brown, *Dreamer-Prophets of the Columbia Plateau,* 31.

The world's leading climate scientists: Sam Meredith, "Fossil Fuels Are Choking Humanity: Major UN Report Sounds the Alarm on Climate Impacts," CNBC, Feb. 28, 2022.

"I wonder," Young Chief said: Trafzer and Beach, "Smohalla, the Washani, and Religion," 314.

"Men who work," Smohalla once said: Trafzer and Beach, "Smohalla, the Washani, and Religion," 320.

Who will save us? Who will act?: The Rt. Rev. Steven Charleston, "To Change History: The Global Covenant," Washington National Cathedral, February 24, 2008, https://tinyurl.com/4rtpsavk.

CHAPTER 5

On New Year's day of 1891: James Mooney, *The Ghost Dance Religion and Wounded Knee* (New York: Dover Publications, 1973), 816–17.

The last words Wovoka said to me: Michael Hittman, *Wovoka and the Ghost Dance* (Lincoln: University of Nebraska Press, 1990), 168.

On this occasion "the sun died": Hittman, *Wovoka and the Ghost Dance*, 17.

The whole world is coming: Mooney, *The Ghost Dance Religion*, 1072.

Wovoka's religion was all the more remarkable: Hittman, *Wovoka and the Ghost Dance*, 98.

All believers were exhorted to make themselves worthy: Mooney, *The Ghost Dance Religion*, 777.

CHAPTER 6

These important prophecies tell us in advance: Thomas E. Mails, *The Hopi Survival Kit* (New York: Penguin Compass, 1997), 173–74.

In the First World there was only Tokpela: There are many variations on the spelling of some Hopi words. For the sake of continuity I have chosen the spellings used by Harold Courlander, *The Fourth World of the Hopis* (Albuquerque: University of New Mexico Press, 1971).

The road to the Upper World was finished: Courlander, *Fourth World of the Hopis*, 24.

That human beings the world over: Mails, *The Hopi Survival Kit*, 239.

"You will go to a certain place": Frank Waters, *Book of the Hopi* (New York: Penguin Books, 1977), 13.

It has height and depth, heat and cold: Waters, *Book of the Hopi,* 21.

With the pristine wisdom granted them: Waters, *Book of the Hopi,* 7.